JAMES KENNETH HAMRICK

ORTHODOX PREACHING

AS THE ORAL ICON OF CHRIST

ORTHODOX PREACHING
AS THE ORAL ICON OF CHRIST
by James Kenneth Hamrick

© 2013, James Kenneth Hamrick

Publishers Maxim Hodak & Max Mendor

© 2015, Orthodox Logos Publishing, The Netherlands

www.orthodoxlogos.com

ISBN: 978-94-92224-01-9

ISBN 978-94-92224-02-6

A master's thesis submitted to the faculty
of the Antiochian House of Studies in partial fulfillment
of the Master of Arts, Balamand University,
Orthodox Patriarchate of Antioch.

JAMES KENNETH HAMRICK

ORTHODOX PREACHING

AS THE ORAL ICON OF CHRIST

ORTHODOX LOGOS PUBLISHING

Contents

To the memory of Archpriest Peter E. Gillquist (July 13, 1938–July 1, 2012), a mentor and fellow laborer in Christ who encouraged me in this endeavor, and who truly appreciated the essential place of preaching in the Orthodox Christian faith.

It is not what he says which is important, but the Spirit which animates it, the Spirit which nourishes his heart and tongue, which gives shape to his sayings and transforms the stones of his speech into icons.

— Archimandrite Vasileios,
*Hymn of Entry: Liturgy and Life
in the Orthodox Church*

Foreword

I had the pleasure to work with Father James Kenneth Hamrick on his Master Thesis entitled, "Orthodox Preaching as the Oral Icon of Christ." This oral icon of Christ is very dear to all the faithful, and forms an essential function of our mission in the Church. It is extremely important to resort to preaching that enables the deprived people to reach the depth of the Orthodox doctrine. This book in hand serves as a very useful tool toward reviving evangelization in the Orthodox Church. Many persons, clergy and laity, will benefit greatly by taking heed to the significant material presented in this book.

Clergy and lay persons alike should consult this book to find inspiration for a clearer grasp of the rich tradition of preaching which is our legacy and an expression of our vital spiritual life in Christ. The insights and contributions of Father James will not go unnoticed or unappreciated. Therefore, clergy looking into proclaiming the Gospel in an Orthodox way will be enriched with this work. He has in view the edification of all our churches in declaring the message of Christ within Liturgical context.

Finally, in return I would extend my heartfelt and unqualified endorsement of this project.

The dissemination of this material should be encouraged throughout the Orthodox world.

V. Rev. Michel Najim, Ph.D.
Saint Nicholas Cathedral, Los Angeles, California

Preface

My appreciation for fine preaching began to develop during my childhood years under the preaching and nurture of my father, the late Reverend Kenneth Carl Hamrick, a Methodist minister for over 30 years. In my own journey of faith from the Protestant tradition to the Orthodox Church, I have been exposed to a broad array of preaching styles: from firebrand revival and Pentecostal preaching, to traditional African American preaching, to the oratorical and solemn style of "high church" preaching, and to the less formal teaching-style of expository preaching that is typical in much of the evangelical Christian tradition. While my own preaching skills have been shaped and influenced by a number of fine preachers from a variety of these traditions, in the years of my pastoral ministry leading up to my conversion to Orthodoxy, I grew increasingly alarmed and dismayed with the trajectory of Christian preaching in our time.

Drifting further and further from its Orthodox roots, the preaching of Christ crucified in our society has given increasing ground to the militant liberalism and pluralism inherent in most mainline seminaries, as well as to the egomaniacal showmanship and antics of preaching charlatans more interested in self-promotion and the emotional manipulation of crowds than in true theological and spiritual integrity. Undeniably, a crisis of preaching presently exists. And while, on the one hand, much of Protestantism has exalted the importance of preaching over the Eucharist, on the other hand, quality preaching in the liturgical traditions, including Holy Orthodoxy, has suffered for a lack of significance and emphasis given to the holy work and discipline of effectively preaching the Good News of God in Christ. This crisis of preaching ranges from otherwise accomplished preaching and oratory within Protestantism plagued by a detachment from the dogmatic and patristic moorings of Orthodoxy to preaching that is Orthodox and theologically correct but that is nevertheless so dry and unimaginative that even the worst sufferer of insomnia is capable of nodding off. Therefore when I set out to complete my master's degree through the Antiochian House of Studies and the University of Balamand, I immediately realized that my thesis research and writing should focus on preaching.

Early on in my research, I discovered an obvious lack of books and articles written on preaching from an Orthodox perspective. Quite frankly, I was stunned. How could the Church of Saint John Chrysostom, Saint Ephraim, Saint Peter Chrysologus and the other great patristic preachers have grown so silent and sidelined within modern scholarship on such a vital aspect of our Christian witness? It would be tantamount to Orthodox theologians having little to say about the Holy Mysteries or the liturgical life of the Church. My own assessment concerning a lack of materials on Orthodox preaching was further reinforced during my recent visit to the Institute for Orthodox Christian Studies at Cambridge University. Professor David Frost, the principal of the Institute, told me that Metropolitan Paul Yazigi (currently an abductee in Syria) had visited a couple of years earlier in order to obtain books and materials on Orthodox preaching for his priests. Professor Frost told me that he had to respond to the Metropolitan, "Your Eminence, I'm afraid we have very little in our library on that subject." Where is the Orthodox voice among the plethora of homiletical research and writings being produced by Protestant and Roman Catholic scholars and practitioners? Yes, we may certainly benefit from the work of our brethren, but surely Holy Orthodoxy has something to offer in the discipline of homiletics.

From my research, I have found that the Orthodox Church indeed has much to offer on the subject of preaching. It is just a matter of appropriating and constituting those materials in order to make them available to the student, scholar, and layman alike. My hope and prayer is that this book will in some small way help to fill that need, though certainly much more work needs to be done. While this book derives from a peer-reviewed academic paper, I am hopeful that it will nonetheless be accessible to not only my fellow clergymen and homiletical scholars, but to all who want to better understand the vital importance of preaching from an Orthodox perspective, to those that wish to better appreciate the fullness of preaching in the context of the whole liturgical and Eucharistic life of grace.

Finally, as we consider the world in which the Apostles were sent to evangelize two millennia ago—a pagan world that was largely hostile to Christianity—we find ourselves and the Church in this "post-Christian" age facing a very similar world with very similar challenges. My research will prayerfully convey the truth that regardless of where we are situated in time and place, and that regardless of what particular style of preaching we might employ in heralding the Gospel of Christ, that it is Orthodox preaching by virtue of its iconic nature which mediates the very presence of our Lord whereby lives may be transformed. As a priest and pastor, the research that I conducted in writing this book has helped to transfigure my own preaching ministry. It has helped me to realize the power of God through the Holy Spirit in making manifest His own divine presence through the proclamation of the Gospel, and to more fully recognize and acknowledge the awesome and weighty importance of our sacred call to faithfully herald the Good News of Jesus Christ. For as proclaimed by Saint Paul, "Woe to me if I do not preach the gospel!" (1 Cor. 9:16, RSV). May we all who have been called to be bearers and heralds of the precious gift of the Gospel approach our work with diligence and faithfulness, with thanksgiving and reverent fear.

Father James K. Hamrick
June 13, 2014

Acknowledgements

I wish to thank my wife, Pamela Hamrick, who has lovingly stood by me during the many years of my formal theological education, especially when it has required the sacrifice of much time and money. I wish to acknowledge the leadership of the Very Rev. Father Joseph Allen, Ph.D. and the knowledge and wisdom imparted by the gifted and devoted faculty and mentors of the Antiochian House of Studies which serves as the solid educational foundation upon which I crafted this thesis. Among those faculty members, I especially wish to thank and acknowledge my first reader, the Very Rev. Father Michel Najim, Ph.D., and my second reader, the Very Rev. Father David Hester, Ph.D. I also want to thank my friend and former mentor, the Rev. Father John Worgul, Ph.D., Dean of Holy Trinity Theological College & Seminary, who led me to the doorsteps of Holy Orthodoxy; and His Grace Bishop Thomas Joseph who brought me safely home to the Church. Finally, in all things, I offer thanksgiving, praise, and glory to the Holy and Undivided Trinity: the Father, Son, and Holy Spirit, from Whom all life and blessings flow.

Introduction

Preaching from the pulpits and platforms of many twenty-first century Christian churches and assemblies has devolved and degraded into something that is considerably removed from the sacred vocation of faithfully proclaiming the Good News of God in Jesus Christ, the Gospel of the crucified, resurrected, and ascended Lord and Savior. Much preaching rather panders to the relativism, consumerism, hedonism, political-correctness, and profound skepticism of our so-called postmodern society. As such, a dominant yet divergent preaching landscape of personality-centered showmanship, syncretistic social gospel, sentimentalism, motivational speaking, philosophizing, and moralizing (perhaps sprinkled with some scriptural references) subsists as the homiletical[1] order of the day in far too many churches. While such preaching may avoid offense, satisfies "itching ears," and at times instructs, delights, and even inspires the listeners, it remains spiritually

---

[1] While the meaning of "homily" (from the Greek *homilia*) and "sermon" (from the Latin *sermō*) denote technical differences in genre and purpose from their usage during the early history of the Church, within the modern vernacular they have become essentially synonymous terms. Therefore for purposes of this paper I use "homily" and its forms interchangeably with "sermon" and its forms.

impotent, incapable of ushering the gathered people into the presence of the Risen Christ where genuine transformation and conversion of life and heart occurs. So how do we address the problem of connecting with the people of this age in a relevant way while remaining faithful and true to the whole Gospel of Christ and to the evangelistic mandate of heralding the Good News? How do we effectively proclaim the Gospel in a manner whereby the preacher is heard and hearts are penetrated?

The answer to our postmodern preaching dilemma lies *not* in Christian fundamentalism and its legalistic preaching that derives from a staunch and rigid biblical literalism. Neither is an effective and satisfying answer found in the atomizing deconstruction of Scripture which tends to occur through a purely expository and deductive approach to preaching, especially when the homiletical task remains distinct and separate from any sense of sacramental and liturgical life. Rather, the ability to effectively engage our postmodern listeners with the truth of the Gospel and to cultivate the possibility of genuine conversion emerges in preaching that is iconic. Specifically, Orthodox preaching that remains faithful to Scripture and to the apostolic and patristic Tradition of biblical interpretation; that is animated by the goal of Orthodox spirituality; and that remains integral to the sacramental and liturgical life of the Church is preaching that truly conveys the Gospel as the oral icon of Christ. It is such iconic preaching that mystically and sacramentally mediates the presence of the Risen Lord in the midst of the assembly. And from such a holy encounter, eyes and ears are opened, lives are interpreted in light of the Gospel, and repentant hearts, enflamed with the Spirit of Christ, cry out in holy fear, adoration, and Eucharistic thanksgiving.

In order to clarify the scope and meaning of Orthodox preaching as the oral icon of Christ, it is first necessary to define what I mean by "Orthodox preaching." For purposes of this paper, I define "Orthodox preaching" as liturgical preaching in the historic, canonical Orthodox Christian Church which adheres to the apostolic and patristic Traditions of preaching and biblical interpretation; or, alternatively, any Trinitarian Christian preaching which maintains an orthodox[1] and patristic theological perspective with respect to the interpretation of Scripture, and to the homiletical task as integral to the formation of the Christian faith in the context of a sacramental and liturgical life of grace. From this definition, I avoid being excessively narrow or exclusive, acknowledging the orthodox preaching and the faithful proclamation of the Gospel by our Christian brethren outside of

---

1 By "orthodox" (small "o"), I refer to a theological perspective which adheres to the essential Trinitarian beliefs of canonical Orthodoxy, especially as articulated by the Nicene-Constantinopolitan Creed, even if from a Christian denomination outside of the canonical Orthodox Church.

the canonical Orthodox Church. On the other hand, this definition of "Orthodox preaching" excludes all preaching that does not adhere to the doctrines, the creeds, and the sacred apostolic and patristic Traditions of the historic Orthodox Church, which unfortunately applies to much of the preaching taking place in many mainline Protestant denominations today, and even within some Catholic churches. "Orthodox preaching" also does not include preaching outside of a liturgical context, such as evangelistic preaching (even though the content may be essentially orthodox in its theology), or any other variety of Christian preaching that is completely divorced from the context of the liturgical life of the Church.

I will rather limit my examination of Orthodox preaching to preaching that is integral to the whole of the sacramental and liturgical life of the Church as possessing the possibility of being iconic, of communicating and sacramentally mediating the presence of Christ in the assembly of the faithful. This is not intended to minimize the value of evangelistic preaching within the mission fields, or catechetical preaching to those desiring to enter the Church, however Orthodox preaching presupposes an Orthodox faith as contextualized, vivified, and enfleshed by the Body of Christ, the Church lived out and made visible and manifest in liturgical and Eucharistic community. Just as not all religious art can be construed as iconic in the Orthodox sense of the term, so not all Christian preaching is iconic.[1] By maintaining this more limited understanding of Orthodox preaching, we are able to focus upon the critical liturgical task of preaching: facilitating the "congregation's recognition of the Lord, their discernment of Jesus Christ in the bread and wine...."[2] It is from this liturgical and sacramental perspective of preaching that we may then begin to carefully examine the iconic nature of Orthodox preaching; that is, what it means in concrete terms for Orthodox preaching to be the oral icon of Christ.

Christian preaching indeed has a varied history, but as Guerric DeBona notes, to follow that history is "to follow a veritable road map of variables that has placed a distinctive weight on the importance of either the text, or the preacher, or the hearer (or, in classical terms, the *logos, ethos, or pathos*), depending on the historical and cultural circumstances."[3] Regardless of the particular historical period and the various emphases of homiletical forms, the unwavering aspects

---

1 Anton Vrame, citing Philip Sherrard, notes that religious art cannot be considered an icon unless "its form derives from spiritual vision, spiritual understanding, and is fused (although not confused) with this spiritual content." Anton C. Vrame, *The Educating Icon: Teaching Wisdom and Holiness in the Orthodox Way* (Brookline, Massachusetts: Holy Cross Orthodox Press, 1999), 13–4.

2 Timothy Clark, "The Function and Task of Liturgical Preaching," *St. Vladimir's Theological Quarterly 45, no. 1* (2001): 44.

3 Guerric DeBona, *Fulfilled in Our Hearing: History and Method of Christian Preaching* (Mahwah, NJ: Paulist Press, 2005), 8.

of Orthodox preaching that has remained universally consistent are the apostolic and patristic lenses through which Scripture is expounded and interpreted; the liturgical context of the preaching and its sacramental nature; and the spiritual end of Orthodox preaching: the leading of the hearers toward the healing of the fractured soul and, ultimately, into union with God. It is from these moorings by which we examine the iconic nature of Orthodox preaching, even as the time and culture conditioned sermonic style, homiletical form, and theological emphasis of preaching spans the centuries and corners of the globe in as rich of a diversity as humanity itself.

The notion of preaching as the oral icon of Christ is certainly something that may effectively resonate with our highly visual and aural postmodern culture, just as Orthodox iconography has served as an effective visual medium of the Gospel over the two millennia of Christendom. "The icon is a type of 'optical Gospel.' It reminds the observer of the Word made flesh and its salvatory role and awakes in him the wish to achieve salvation in Christ."[1] Drawing from this understanding of iconography, it is an easy step to think in terms of preaching the Gospel as the presentation of an oral icon, especially when sermons are preached as word pictures and as the

---

1 Theodor Nikolaou, "The Place of the Icon in the Liturgical Life of the Orthodox Church," *Greek Orthodox Theological Review* 35, no. 4 (1990): 325.

listeners are receiving and processing the spoken word as images within their own minds' eye. These strong parallels between visual image and word image as conveyers of truth and the transcendent reality beyond the signs themselves lend credence and support for the reasons that I approach the study and discipline of Orthodox preaching from an iconological perspective. It is from such a vantage point that I propose an answer lies to the problem of connecting our postmodern culture with the immutable truth of the Gospel. Such a relativistic culture is largely closed to bare propositional truth, no matter how cogently and logically presented. The same culture, however, is ripe for receiving images and for experientially and inductively appropriating the Gospel as its own (the ability to reject Christ notwithstanding). It is therefore from this iconological dimension that we examine the key aspects of Orthodox preaching which remains closely aligned to the preparation, presentation, and spirituality of Orthodox icons.

In Chapter 1 we will consider the "preparation of the icon" as we examine the work of biblical interpretation by the preacher and the rendering of the Gospel by means of a Christological hermeneutic. We will endeavor to demonstrate how the patristic methodologies of typology and *theōria* served as solid, well-grounded exegetical tools which are still necessary for a thoroughly Orthodox and

Christological understanding of Scripture today. It is indeed this patristic and Christological approach to biblical interpretation that reflects the Orthodox understanding of God's self-revelation. In the words of Florovsky, "The fullness of revelation is Christ Jesus."[1]

Chapter 2 considers the "placement of the icon" as the liturgical setting of Orthodox preaching and the place of preaching in the larger context of sacramentally mediating the presence of the Risen Lord in the gathering of God's faithful, especially as encountered in the Eucharist. It is in this context that preaching serves the primary reality of "Christ in the assembly, the People of God."[2] And from this primary reality we will examine the sacramental role and function of the liturgical sermon as that which integrates and unites Word and Sacrament, for as Thomas Hopko asserts, "There is no Christian liturgy without God's Word."[3]

Chapter 3 moves into the work of "presenting the icon," that is, the revelatory art of preaching whereby the truth of the Gospel is artfully and imaginatively

---

1 Georges Florovsky, *Bible, Church, Tradition: An Eastern Orthodox View* (Belmont, Massachusetts: Nordland Publishing Company, 1972), 24.

2 United States Conference of Catholic Bishops. *Fulfilled in Your Hearing: The Homily in the Sunday Assembly* (Washington, DC: United States Conference of Catholic Bishops, 1982), 4.

3 Thomas Hopko, "The Liturgical Sermon," *St. Vladimir's Theological Quarterly* 41, no. 2–3 (1997): 177.

proclaimed in a manner that engages the listeners with word pictures which assists them to recognize Christ in their midst, to interpret their own lives in the light of the Good News, and to move them toward repentance and a desire for holy imitation. In this chapter, we will examine the effectiveness of inductive preaching as typified by the parabolic preaching of Jesus. We will also consider this inductive and iconic approach to preaching through select examples of St. John Chrysostom's homilies which artfully incorporated the use of Pauline portraitures as a method for inducing imitation. From the Western Church, we will survey some examples of homilies by St. Peter Chrysologus who skillfully mastered the use of verbal images and word pictures in his preaching as a method of making the truth of the Gospel accessible and relevant to his listeners.

Finally, Chapter 4 presents preaching from the aspect of "engaging the icon," that is, as locating its ultimate center and role in tandem with Orthodox spirituality. Preaching that is truly iconic entails the prophetic dimension of the proclamation the Gospel. It is from the aspect of the sacred office of the clergy *as prophet* by which the listeners are moved beyond the mere spoken word as sign and symbol according to its grammatical and literal meaning into the eternal and transcendent realm of the Divine where the healing and restoration of the broken and diffused soul may occur. In this chapter we will examine how iconic preaching as a "window into the heavenly world"[1] transports its listeners to a place of mystical anagogy; to a place of divine and holy encounter which results in true, godly repentance necessary for the purification of the heart and for becoming, by grace, "partakers of the divine nature."[2] In short, where preaching begins with *theōria* as a contemplative Christological hermeneutic methodology, so it ends with *theōria*, the vision of God produced by the mystical encounter with the Risen Lord via Orthodox preaching, the oral icon of Christ.

---

1 Linette Martin, *Sacred Doorways: A Beginner's Guide to Icons* (Brewster, Massachusetts: Paraclete Press, 2002), 78.

2 2 Pet. 1:4, RSV.

Chapter 1

PREPARING THE ICON:
TOWARD A CHRISTOLOGICAL
HERMENEUTIC

> If we are truly to understand Christian preaching, we must see Jesus Christ at its center. First we must see Jesus as the fulfillment of generations of preaching and teaching that went before him, and second we must see Jesus as the type, or perhaps prototype, of generations of preaching that have followed him. He is both the pattern of preaching and the gospel to be preached.
> — Hughes Oliphant Old,
> *The Reading and Preaching of Scripture in the Worship of the Christian Church, The Biblical Period*

Since Christ is the source, subject, and end of Christian preaching, and also stands as the fullness of God's self-revelation, then it is quite appropriate that the preacher's work of discerning a "word from the Lord" begins from a Christological center. Preparing the oral icon of Christ necessarily entails a prayerful and contemplative approach to Scripture which in Orthodoxy has often been proclaimed as the verbal icon of Christ.[1] The Bible as the verbal icon of Christ serves as the principal source of sacred Tradition from which the preacher prepares his homily which will serve as the oral icon of Christ. However, the task of accurately interpreting a divinely inspired human literary work that spans many centuries and cultures is no easy accomplishment. And with the application of the historical-critical method which is taught in many seminaries today, the task of biblical interpretation has potentially become even more daunting. The presentation of an accurate and effective oral icon of Christ in preaching presupposes an accurate and effective rendering of Scripture. It is therefore imperative that the preacher gets it right; and that certainty of accuracy and faithfulness to the Gospel text only exists as the preacher, illumined by the Spirit of Christ, interprets Scripture with the mind of the Church. It indeed follows that a hermeneutic appropriate to the Church, the Body of Christ, is necessarily a Christological hermeneutic since, as Florovsky notes, "The true theme of the whole Bible

---

1   Veselin Kesich, "The Verbal Icon of Christ," Orthodox Research Institute, accessed July 16, 2013, http://www.orthodoxresearchinstitute.org/articles/dogmatics/kesich_verbal_icon.htm.

is Christ and his Church, not nations or societies, nor the sky and the earth."[1]

Accurate and faithful biblical interpretation does not proceed from mere academic rigor and literary criticism or from creative innovation, but from creative adherence to the apostolic and patristic Traditions of exegesis in submission to the authority of the Church so that a proper spiritual sense of Scripture may be discerned. Emmanuel Hatzidakis argues this point from the placement of the sermon in the Liturgy: "By establishing the sermon immediately after the Readings from the Holy Scripture, we see that Church does not leave the interpretation of the Holy Scripture up to each one of us, but wants to make sure that our interpretation is that of the Church, who wants to guide her children always to the truth."[2] In a similar vein, Florovsky asserts, "Revelation is preserved in the Church. Therefore, the Church is the proper and primary interpreter of revelation."[3] Beyond the preservation of divine revelation, Florovsky stresses the coherence in the body of traditional doctrine in the Church which "can be apprehended and understood only in the living context of faith, by which I mean in a personal communion with the personal God. ...

---

[1] Florovsky, 35.

[2] Emmanuel Hatzidakis, *The Heavenly Banquet: Understanding the Divine Liturgy* (Columbia, MO: Orthodox Witness, 2008), 147.

[3] Florovsky, 25.

For Christ is not a text but a living Person, and he abides in his body, the church."[1] The preparation of the oral icon must therefore proceed from a Christological hermeneutic that derives from and is informed by the Church and its Orthodox Tradition. The patristic exegetical Tradition of the Church is perhaps no better embodied than in the writings Saint Irenaeus of Lyons. Arguing against the heresies of the Valentinians who distorted Scripture toward their own impious ends, Saint Irenaeus metaphorically describes the Scriptures as a mosaic; a "beautiful image of a king... constructed by some skillful artist out of precious jewels...."[2] The clear implication is that these holy Scriptures as a beautiful mosaic of Christ the King may only be rightly divided and interpreted by the preacher as he understands and acknowledges what is before him, and as he interprets with the same divinely inspired creativity which fashioned the mosaic in the first place. Vladislav Andrejev states, "Iconic creativity issues out of the entire church's dogmatic heritage, which is founded on divine revelation."[3] This certainly

---

1 Ibid., 14.

2 Saint Irenaeus of Lyons, *Ante-Nicene Fathers: The Apostolic Fathers with Justin Martyr and Irenaeus*, ed. Alexander Roberts & James Donaldson, Vol. 1 (Peabody, Massachusetts: Hendrickson Publishers, Inc., 1999), 326.

3 Vladislav Andrejev, "Art and Religion: Creativity and the Meaning of Image from the Perspective of the Orthodox Icon," *Theology Toady* 61 (2004): 59.

applies to the iconic creativity that is involved with the interpretative work of the preacher as he sets out to prepare the oral icon of Christ in a homily.

Before proceeding with an examination of the tools and methodologies of Orthodox exegesis and those particular aspects which characterizes a Christological hermeneutic, the question regarding the place of modern literary criticism in Orthodox exegesis should be considered. While the modern historical-critical method of biblical interpretation may certainly serve the preacher well in understanding something about authorial intent, the original audience, the historical context, and literary form and construction of the biblical text, from an Orthodox perspective, such a methodology is never an end of itself. Instead, it is merely a tool which serves the interpreter rather than the interpreter serving the methodology. The modern historical-critical method represents a shift from the moorings of patristic exegesis, and is therefore potentially problematic, particularly as it is applied as a stand-alone interpretative methodology divorced from the mind of the Church. Craig Satterlee argues:

> While the patristic approach to Scripture provided a sort of conceptual unity to the Church even while allowing for significant differences, the historical-critical method has produced fragmentation, rendering Scripture unintelligible to anyone except trained experts in the history, language, culture, and

beliefs of the centuries and peoples spanned by the Bible, thereby distancing the Church from its Scriptures....The problem is not that the historical-critical method is in use; the problem arises when it displaces all other methods and comes to be seen as an end in itself, the final step in the process of interpreting Scripture.[1]

While the modern historical-critical method may have value, it clearly becomes problematic when the interpretative method operates apart from the Church and Her sacred and patristic Traditions of biblical interpretation. To labor under a purely empirical and scientific approach to biblical interpretation is to miss the divine nature of Scripture (as well as the divinely inspired work of interpretation) and to consequently succumb to the spirit of this age, as articulated by Raniero Cantalamessa:

...we in the West have witnessed a massive relapse into the letter and flesh. The prevailing rationalism requires Christianity to present its message in dialectical form, that is, subjecting every aspect of it to discussion and research, so that it can fit into the general, philosophically acceptable picture of an

---

[1] Craig Alan Satterlee, *Ambrose of Milan's Method of Mystagogical Preaching* (Collegeville, Minnesota: The Liturgical Press, 2002), 324.

effort on the part of human nature to understand itself and the universe.[1]

Certainly, such acquiescence embodies the warning conveyed by St. Paul to the Church in Colossae: "See to it that no one makes a prey of you by philosophy and empty deceit, according to human tradition, according to the elemental spirits of the universe, and not according to Christ."[2] Indeed, it is a Christological hermeneutic which St. Paul implies as a response to the vain and empty rationalism intrinsic to the world and the academy. In fact, St. Paul's phrase, "according to Christ," signifies the heart of Orthodox exegesis.

Grounded in the very Person of Jesus Christ, the apostolic and patristic approach to biblical interpretation "according to Christ" serves as the unifying center to the hermeneutical work of the Orthodox preacher. Robert Louis Wilken distinguishes this patristic approach from a mere philosophical worldview: "For the Greeks, God was the conclusion of an argument, the end of a search for an ultimate explanation, an inference from the structure of the universe to a first cause. For Christian thinkers, God was the starting point,

---

1 Raniero Cantalamessa, *The Mystery of God's Word*, trans. Alan Neame (Collegeville, Minnesota: The Liturgical Press, 1994), 57.

2 Col. 2:8, RSV.

and Christ the icon that displays the face of God."[1] Inarguably, Wilken's reference to Christ as the icon of God hearkens from the explicit Pauline teaching concerning Christ as the image of the person (*hypostasis*) of God.[2] So it is Christ, the icon of God, which serves as the starting point and the spiritual vision for the work of the preacher who endeavors to craft an oral icon of Christ through preaching and the faithful interpretation of Scripture. Indeed, it is the very Person of Jesus who gives us the Christological hermeneutic utilized in the apostolic and patristic approach to scriptural interpretation and preaching, as indicated by Hughes Oliphant Old, "It was Jesus himself, as summed up in the story of the Emmaus road, who opened to his disciples the Scriptures (Luke 24:32). It was Jesus who established the Christian interpretation of the Scriptures, and it was from Jesus that the apostles learned this interpretation."[3] This Christological method of interpretation, as a matter

---

1 Robert Louis Wilken, *The Spirit of Early Christian Thought: Seeking the Face of God* (New Haven & London: Yale University Press, 2003), 15

2 "He is the image of the invisible God...." (Col. 1:15, NKJV), & "who being the brightness of His glory and the express image of His person [*hypostasis*]..." (Heb. 1:3, NKJV)

3 Hughes Oliphant Old, *The Reading and Preaching of Scriptures in the Worship of the Christian Church, The Biblical Period*, Vol. 1 (Grand Rapids, Michigan: William B. Eerdmans Publishing Company, 1998), 251.

of devoted succession of the Faith, passed from the apostles to the patristic age of the Church, and to the Orthodox exegesis of our day. It is this Christological method which derives from the iconic nature of the apostolic witness, as Florovsky explains, "The Evangelists and the Apostles were no chroniclers. It was not their mission to keep the full record of all that Jesus had done, day by day, year by year. They describe his life and relate to his works, so as to give us his image: an historic, and yet divine image. It is no portrait, but rather an ikon — but surely an historic ikon, an image of the Incarnate Lord."[1]

From this historic "ikon" of Christ, we now consider the particulars of patristic hermeneutics, passed on from the apostolic age, which abides as the foundation upon which our Orthodox exegesis is built. To adopt a patristic view of biblical interpretation is, in essence, to adopt a Christological hermeneutic. Such a Christological hermeneutic is not simply the lenses through which we conduct the work of biblical interpretation, but additionally signifies the goal and direction of the work which is consistent with the whole of salvation history. John Breck elaborates, "As the ultimate *source*, *interpreter* and *fulfillment* of Scripture, and therefore of theology itself, the Spirit thus guides the Church 'into all the Truth,' towards its *telos*, its final consummation in

---

1 Florovsky, 25.

the Kingdom of God."[1] It is from such a worldview that the Fathers of the Church continued to develop the methodology of scriptural interpretation established by Christ Himself. In the course of the Church's theological maturation and "coming of age," the particular patristic methodologies which characterized the Christological hermeneutic of the Fathers incorporated the use of typology and *theōria* — typology as a means of viewing the whole of Scripture and salvation history from a thoroughly Christological perspective, and *theōria* as a means of contemplatively discerning and discovering the spiritual sense (*sensus spiritualis*) of the text.

In the first centuries of the Church, typology and *theōria* were not universally embraced as hermeneutic methodologies. The competing views of biblical interpretation as embodied by the School of Alexandria and the School of Antioch reflected the tensions between Hebrew and Greek influences. Hughes Oliphant Old distinguishes between those influences and articulates the importance of typology for biblical interpretation:

The greatest difference between Hebrew typology and Greek allegory is that Hebrew typology is an integral part of the way Scripture is understood.

1 John Breck, *The Power of the Word in the Worshipping Church* (Crestwood, New York: St. Vladimir's Seminary Press, 1986), 47.

It is part of the dynamic of promise and fulfillment that is of the essence of the covenant relationship.... True biblical typology takes place in Scripture itself. It is integral to the process of Scripture interpreting Scripture.[1]

The gift of the Antiochene School was its hermeneutic methodologies of typology and *theōria* which ultimately won the day. Even though allegory continued to be utilized as a method of interpretation within certain enclaves of the early Church, it would eventually be eclipsed within Orthodox thought by a more Christological and less innovative approach to Scripture, which is also more consistent with the reality of salvation history and its eschatological nature. Florovsky explains:

For an "allegorist" the "images" he interprets are reflections of a pre-existing prototype, or even images of some eternal or abstract "truth." They are pointing to something that is outside of the time. On the contrary, typology is oriented towards the future. The "types" are anticipations, *pre*-figurations; their "prototype" is still to come. Typology is thus an historical method, more than a philological one. It presupposes and implies intrinsically the reality of history, directed and guided by God. It is organically

---

1 Old, 339.

connected with the idea of the covenant. Here the past, the present and the future are linked in a unity of divine purpose, and the purpose was Christ. Therefore typology has emphatically a Christological meaning (the Church is included here, as the Body and the Bride of Christ).[1]

Breck also proffers that typology "is based upon the premise that historical events in Israel's history are related in terms either of 'promise and fulfillment' or of 'prototype to antitype.'"[2] For these reasons, typology emerged over allegory as a thoroughly Christological approach to biblical interpretation. Besides the forging of a perspective of salvation history in terms of the Incarnation and the Cross of Christ, typology brings movement, coherence, and unity to the entire biblical witness.

The distinction between the two Testaments belongs itself to the unity of the Biblical revelation. The two Testaments are to be carefully distinguished, never to be confused. Yet they are organically linked together, not as two systems only, but primarily in the person of Christ. Jesus the Christ belongs to both. He is the fulfiller of the old dispensation and by the same act that he fulfills the old, "the Law

---

1 Florovsky, 32.

2 Breck, 39.

and the prophets," he inaugurates the new, and thereby becomes the ultimate fulfiller of both, i.e. of the whole. He is the very centre of the Bible, just because his is the *archē* and the *telos* — the beginning and the end.[1]

Typology therefore serves well the Christological hermeneutic, the view of salvation history "according to Christ" which delineates the essence of Orthodox biblical exegesis.

However, typology as an Orthodox methodology of biblical interpretation does not function independently. Rather, the "soul" of typology is known as *theōria*, the prayerful and contemplative vision of God through Christ which enables the interpreter to discern and discover the higher spiritual sense of the text. As Old notes, "The New Testament does not interpret the Old Testament allegorically, but it does find in the Old Testament higher and more profound meanings. This higher meaning of Scripture Diodore calls *theoria;* it is the 'spiritual sense' of the Antiochene School."[2] Just as Scripture is not merely a human work, but rather a compilation of sacred writings by human authors inspired and guided by the Holy Spirit, so

---

1 Florovsky, 22–3.

2 Hughes Oliphant Old, *The Reading and Preaching of Scriptures in the Worship of the Christian Church, The Patristic Age*, Vol. 2 (Grand Rapids, Michigan: William B. Eerdmans Publishing Company, 1998), 178.

the interpretation of Scripture is necessarily a divine-human work. "As a hermeneutic method, *theōria* was based upon two fundamental presuppositions: that Scripture is uniformly inspired by God, and that typology offers the key to its right interpretation."[1] The exercise of the typological methodology by means of human cognition is animated through divine assistance — it is the contemplative and spiritual vision of God in Christ which brings supernatural insight to the work of reading, studying, and interpreting the Holy Scriptures.

> *Theōria* or contemplative vision, then, is as essential to the exegete as it was to the biblical authors.... *theōria* includes both the inspired vision by which the exegete discerns the spiritual sense of the text, and the attitude of contemplation which is an essential condition for receiving that vision. *Theōria* thus informs and guides every aspect of exegesis.[2]

Preparing the oral icon of Christ is born out of the interpretive and exegetical work of the preacher in synergistic union with the divine work of God in providing spiritual vision and contemplative insight. While *theōria* is both spiritual vision and the disposition necessary for spiritual vision, *theōria*

---

1 Breck, 95.

2 Ibid., 111.

entails a broad expanse of divine activity in relation to the Christological hermeneutic. Breck details these specific aspects:

> This hermeneutic activity of the Spirit of Truth involves three interrelated elements: 1) the historical event; 2) proclamation of the soteriological significance of that event by the biblical author; and 3) interpretation and actualization of that proclamation by the Church in each new generation. The work of the Spirit consists in *supplying* the event with typological significance and in leading the prophetic, apostolic or later witness to *discern* that significance and then to *proclaim* and *transmit* it as an element of Church Tradition.[1]

From the place of endeavoring to discern the topological significance of the Scriptures, the preacher must submit himself to the work of the Divine. In fact, Breck argues that the so-called "hermeneutical circle" remains closed to the exegete unless his work is born out of a faith which presupposes the work of the Holy Spirit as "the principal agent in the work of interpretation."[2] Within the Orthodox theological tradition, the exegete becomes *theodidaktos* (one taught by God) whereby "the preacher realizes that

---

1 Breck, 44.

2 Ibid., 46.

his message is not his own; it is given to him by the Holy Spirit."[1] In essence, *theōria* as a hermeneutic method involves worship. "To interpret Scripture spiritually is to enter into genuine worship, according to Ephrem. It is to stand before the presence of God in awe and wonder and, hearing his Word, to be transformed by that Word in the image of the Son of God. The spiritual interpretation is something which is experienced. It is to experience both justification and sanctification."[2] It is through *theōria* as a place of worship by which the preacher becomes an active participant in divine revelation and thus becomes an agent of divine transformation. "To recover the proper doctrinal and doxological dimensions of Scripture, *the exegete himself must participate in the process of divine revelation.* He must submit himself and his skill to the guiding influence of the Holy Spirit, if his efforts are to bear fruit for faith and salvation."[3]

In our age of innovation and relativism in which the task of biblical interpretation is often left to personal fancy and the popery of the individual believer, Orthodox preaching abides as a sentinel to the "faith which was once for all delivered to the saints."[4]

---

1 Anthony Coniaris, *Preaching the Word of God* (Brookline, Massachusetts: Holy Cross Orthodox Press, 1983), 49.

2 Old, *The Patristic Age*, 259–60.

3 Breck, 45.

4 Jude 1:3, RSV.

Orthodox preaching as the oral icon of Christ points to a compelling way back to the Christological center of the Apostles and the Fathers. It is from this place that Orthodox preaching finds the source and genesis of its iconic nature, as indicated by Paul Tarazi, "It is there [in the prophets and the Apostles] that we will find the face of our Lord in its pristine beauty, and after having met Him, be able to convey Him — even without quotations! — to our hungry and thirsty brothers and sisters. There, in the biblical text, is the truest, most historical, most lively, and most accurate icon of His."[1] And while the preacher labors in the work of exegesis within the iconic qualities of Scripture, the historical-critical method of modernity is not necessarily jettisoned. It is however relegated to its proper place — subservient to the Christological hermeneutic which is guided and informed by typology and enlivened by *theōria*, the contemplative vision of God. As such, the exegetical task of the preacher remains properly grounded, and preaching may emerge as iconic. Robert Arida notes, "The icon, like the Gospel, transmits the language of the Church. Both the statements of the Gospel and the statements of the icon emerge from the Church's collective memory (ἀνάμνησις) kept alive in the

---

1 Paul N. Tarazi, *Orthodox Synthesis: The Unity of Theological Thought*, ed. Joseph J. Allen (Crestwood, New York: St. Vladimir's Seminary Press, 1981), 179.

Holy Spirit and retained in worship."[1] It is from this place of worship that *theōria* as a hermeneutic methodology is ultimately located, and as we will see in Chapter 2, it is also in the context of liturgical worship that the oral icon of Christ, as presented in preaching, is properly placed.

---

1 Robert M. Arida, "Second Nicaea: The Vision of the New Man and New Creation in the Orthodox Icon," *Theology Today* 61 (2004): 423.

Chapter 2

PLACEMENT OF THE ICON:
THE LITURGICAL SETTING
OF PREACHING

> Our Protestant brethren have a great
> deal to teach us about the central place
> of the Word of God in Christian life and
> missions. As Orthodox, however, our
> responsibility is to insist upon the fact that
> the true place of the Word — its exegesis
> as well as its proclamation — is within
> the liturgical, sacramental community
> of the Church.
> — John Breck, *The Power of the Word in
> the Worshipping Church*

As detailed in the previous chapter, the
interpretation of Scripture through a Christological
hermeneutic is a key aspect of preparing to preach, of
preparing the oral icon of Christ. However, preaching

is far more than simply having something to say about what the Scriptures express. Rather, Orthodox preaching in the fullest sense is really about the divine initiative of God revealing Himself through His Word which is proclaimed by the preacher — it is a supernatural event within the assembly of the faithful which, by sacramental grace, is made manifest and heard through the medium of human speech and hearing.[1] As indicated by Charles Miller, "Preaching is, like Jesus, divine and human. The divine word comes to us clothed in human words."[2] This theophanic event however is not something that occurs simply because someone is giving voice to the printed Word, as though the preacher were magically incanting divinely inspired words in order to conjure up the presence of the Divine. Rather, God, by grace, makes Himself mystically present through the spoken Word within the larger context of liturgical and Eucharistic worship, all animated by the divine work of the Holy Spirit. Just as

---

1   Following the sacramental theology of Karl Rahner, Paul Janowiak quotes Rahner, saying that "Christ is the primal sacramental word of God" and that the Church is "the abiding presence of this very Christ." Janowiak argues that this "interconnectedness between God's word and the human word is essential." Paul Janowiak, *The Holy Preaching: The Sacramentality of the Word in the Liturgical Assembly* (Collegeville, Minnesota: The Liturgical Press, 2000), 41.

2   Charles E. Miller, *Ordained to Preach: A Theology and Practice of Preaching* (Eugene, Oregon: Wipf and Stock Publishers, 2003), 7.

careful consideration must be given to the appropriate placement of icons in the Church and at home, so the placement of preaching as the oral icon of Christ finds its rightful place within the worshipping Eucharistic community of Faith. And as we will examine, the locus of preaching in the Divine Liturgy functions to convey and to reinforce the essential coherence and symbiosis which exists between the Word and Sacrament.

While ample biblical precedence certainly exists for evangelistic preaching outside of an immediate liturgical context, including the first Christian sermon preached by St. Peter on the Day of Pentecost,[1] Orthodox preaching in the scope of which we are currently examining it remains integral to the liturgical and Eucharistic life of the Church. In fact, the archetypal pattern for this connection between Word and Sacrament predates Pentecost and derives from the post-resurrection account of Jesus' appearance to the two disciples on the road to Emmaus.[2] In this account not only does Jesus establish the Church's method for interpreting the Scriptures, but He also links together Word and Sacrament in a manner whereby the expounding of Scriptures prepares His hearers for the opening of their eyes and the recognition of the Risen Lord in "the breaking of the bread."[3] Christ

---

[1] See Acts 2:14–36.

[2] See Luke 24:13–35.

[3] Luke 24:35, RSV.

Himself gives us the example of this two-fold shape of the Liturgy which became the pattern for Christian liturgical worship. Coniaris notes, "According to the Church Fathers, there are two communions in the Liturgy. We commune first with Christ as the word of God (Liturgy of the Word), and then with Christ as the bread of life (Liturgy of the Faithful). In both communions we partake of Christ. First we break the word of God, then we break the bread of life."[1]

This duality of worship maintains the appropriate balance and interdependence between the evangelistic mission of the Church and the sacramental grace of God imparted through the Holy Mysteries. Word and Sacrament do not exist as mutually exclusive (as an "either-or"), nor as an independent bifurcation whereby one may easily be dissected from the other. Rather, an interdependent symbiosis between liturgical preaching and the Eucharist necessarily exists. Old indicates that it "is through both the preached Word and the Lord's Supper that we have covenant fellowship with the incarnate Word. It is in both together that Christ is truly present."[2] *Fulfilled in Your Hearing* asserts, "In the Eucharistic celebration the homily points to the presence of God in people's lives and then leads a congregation into the Eucharist, providing, as it were, the motive for celebrating the Eucharist in this time and

---

1 Coniaris, 3.

2 Old, *The Biblical Period*, 162.

place."[1] The Conference of Catholic Bishops further emphasizes this relationship of interdependence:

> The very meaning and function of the homily is determined by its relation to the liturgical action of which it is part. It flows from the Scriptures which are read at the liturgical celebration, or, more broadly, from the Scriptures which undergird its prayers and actions, and it enables the congregation to participate in the celebration of faith.... A homily presupposes faith.[2]

Timothy Clark argues that the "fullness of Christian worship is only conceivable when the linguistic Word of Jesus Christ and the physical manifestation of that Word are understood to subsist in each other. Only when each component of the liturgy is performed in view of the other, is it possible to fulfill completely its sacramental function."[3] In fact, it is the homily which serves as the mechanism by which Word and Sacrament are united.[4] And in this convergence of the revelation of God through the preached Word and the revelation of God through the Sacraments (as the participation in the uncreated

---

1 United States Conference of Catholic Bishops, 23.

2 Ibid., 17.

3 Clark, 26.

4 Ibid., 26.

energies of God), the fullness of Christian worship is maintained.

> In authentic Orthodox experience, the Word comes to its fullest expression within a sacramental context. Whether proclaimed through Scripture reading and preaching, or sung in the form of antiphons (psalms) and dogmatic hymns (festal toparia, the Monogenês and Credo), the Word of God is primarily communicated — expressed and received — by the ecclesial act of *celebration*, and in particular, celebration of the eucharistic mystery.[1]

Satterlee expounds on the patristic view of the integrity of Word and Sacrament and the relationship of mutual interdependence, and how that translates at a practical level in Christian living:

> ...the Fathers sought a dynamic whole not only in Scripture but also between Scripture and the Christian life. Scripture and Church are united by the Church's experience of Christ's presence in baptism and Eucharist. Baptism changes who Christians are and Scripture provides the language, description, and images that illuminate what that change looks like in the lives of believers. Receiving the Eucharist makes the neophytes different;

---

1 Breck, 17–8.

Scripture gives the framework for how to live with this difference. At the same time, the life and experience of the Church determine what the Scriptures mean. The sacraments are at the heart of the Church's life and experience; therefore, baptism and Eucharist provide the context for interpreting Scripture. From this convergence of liturgy and Bible, of Scripture and sacrament, the Fathers derived their images and metaphors and language for describing and encouraging the Christian life.[1]

In having its source in the very Person of Christ, a certain consubstantiation exists between Word and Sacrament such that to divest one from the other, or to exalt one above the other, is to skew the appropriate theological and sacramental relationship and to ultimately detract from the pattern of worship which God has established.

Since preaching presupposes a community of faith, a community of baptized believers, the homily not only directs the listeners toward the Eucharist, but it also points them back to their Baptism. As indicated by Todd Townshend, "This reaching back to the Baptism of the members, renewing in them the sense of membership in the *ecclesia*, and leading forward to the action of the Eucharist, places preaching between font and altar. The Word and Sacrament find their unity

---

[1] Satterlee, 326.

in the action of the ordained minister of the *ecclesia*."[1] From an Orthodox perspective, this unity derives from the charismatic ministry and sacred office of the local bishop who, when acting liturgically in the midst of the assembly, represents the fullness and the catholicity of the Church. In the absence of the bishop, it is the priest acting under the authority of the bishop (and in the person of the bishop) whereby a sacramental grace is bestowed toward the revelation of God. This sacramental grace, however, is not limited to the liturgical actions of the priest in the Sacraments, but is present in the ministry of the Word as well. Coniaris notes, "Preaching is a reincarnation of the word of God. When the priest mounts the pulpit, the word of God becomes flesh again."[2] As preaching lies between Baptism and the Eucharist and points to each, it serves to illuminate its own sacramental nature while upholding the unity and necessary balance between the Word and Sacrament.

Preaching as the oral icon of Christ becomes misplaced whenever the balance and symbiosis between Word and Sacrament is not maintained. William Skudlarek indicates, "Preaching at its finest is preaching that is biblically centered, directed to the real questions of people, and taken up in worship. The

---

1 Todd Townshend, *The Sacramentality of Preaching: Homiletical Uses of Louis-Marie Chauvet's Theology of Sacramentality* (New York, New York: Peter Lang Publishing, Inc., 2009), 13

2 Coniaris, 11.

past generation of Roman Catholics and Protestants experienced, for the most part, a form of worship that was a mere torso — a sacramental service without preaching, a preaching service without the sacrament."[1] Within much of Protestantism, there exists a prevailing tendency toward the exaltation of preaching over the Eucharist. William Willimon assesses the state of affairs within his own sector of Christianity:

> Protestantism has elevated the sermon as the supreme religious endeavor. In most Protestant worship, the focus is on the pulpit. The cleric becomes a "preacher" rather than a priest or prophet. Talk about Christianity replaces Christianity. Listening to a sermon becomes a virtue in itself.... Feeling about a sermon replaces response to a sermon. The sermon, ironically, becomes a means whereby the listener protects himself against the radical demands of the faith.[2]

From an Orthodox perspective, Breck argues how "too frequently...the concept of the 'Word of God' in Reformed tradition has been reduced to the canonical Scriptures or even to the sermon, as though one or the other possessed in and of itself the capacity to transmit

---

1   William Skudlarek, *The Word in Worship: Preaching in a Liturgical Context* (Nashville: Abingdon Press, 1981), 9.

2   William H. Willimon, "Kierkegaard on Preachers Who Become Poets," *Worship* 49, no. 2 (1975): 109.

knowledge of God and to establish communion with Him."[1] Breck further elaborates how Protestantism's emphasis on the written Word which grew from a skewed hermeneutic has detracted from the hypostatic nature of Word and Sacrament:

> From an Orthodox point of view…the Protestants did not go far enough towards elaborating a truly "spiritual" hermeneutic. By isolating pneumatology from ecclesiology, they lost sight of the proper context in which the message of the Holy Scriptures should be interpreted and proclaimed. The liturgy and sacraments were no longer seen to be essential means for actualizing and appropriating the Word of God. This vital work was to be accomplished through preaching alone. The very expression "Word of God" was restricted to the Bible and its exposition. "The Word" thus became a purely verbal phenomenon. As a result, the *hypostatic character of the Word* — the personal reality of the divine Logos — became obscured by an exaggerated accent placed on *words*: the written and spoken words of Scripture and preaching.[2]

Ironically, despite the skewed emphasis on preaching and biblical exegesis, this purely verbal approach to

---

1 Breck, 14.

2 Breck, 32.

the Word of God by many segments of Protestantism has done violence to its own evangelical cause. The Word preached apart from any sense of its sacramental character deriving from its place in the Liturgy results in the diminishment of the iconic nature of preaching and its power to mediate the presence of God whereby hearts encounter the saving grace of God made manifest in the fullness of the Good News of God in Christ. Fred Craddock acknowledges something of the sacramental nature of preaching when he states that "preaching is understood as making present and appropriate to the hearers the revelation of God."[1] When the fullness of God's revelation, resident in both Word *and* Sacrament, is diminished through the divestiture of preaching from the Holy Mysteries, then preaching has lost much of its power. As asserted by Breck, "To perceive the essentially sacramental character of the Word, then, we first have to pass beyond a strictly verbal notion of the Word and rediscover its *dynamic* quality, its revelatory and saving *power* as an instrument of divine will."[2]

The antithesis to Protestantism's exaltation of preaching over the Sacraments is the tendency toward dead sacramentalism within liturgical traditions. While the Sacraments may stand alone, they are nonetheless expressed in the kerygmatic and evangelical mandate

---

[1] Fred B. Craddock, *Preaching* (Nashville: Abingdon Press, 1985), 51.

[2] Breck, 15.

of the Church to herald the Gospel. Coniaris states, "In preaching God literally communicates his word through us....The very sacraments themselves cannot exist without preaching, since there is no sacrament without faith and no faith without preaching. Ephraim the Syrian goes so far as to say that 'He [Jesus] entered the womb [of Mary] through her ear' at the Annunciation."[1]

Eusebius Stephanou, addressing what he perceives as the problem of dead formalism within some corners of the Orthodox Church, offers a remedy:

> ...the corrective to dead formalism that is fomented by a crude sacramentalism is the restoration of the vital importance of the diaconia of the word of God. There must be a balance between the sacraments and the word ministry. We need both. They are both of equal importance. But the active ministry of the word helps to prevent the sacraments from deteriorating into religious routine and barren ritual.[2]

It is out of the evangelical witness of the Church and Her faithfulness in proclaiming the whole Gospel of Christ by which the signs of Sacrament take on

---

1 Coniaris, 2.

2 Eusebius A. Stephanou, *Sacramentalized But Not Evangelized* (Destin, FL: St. Symeon the New Theologian Press, 2005), 88.

true significance for the faithful. That is why a Liturgy without a homily or with the homily appended to the end of the Liturgy is a form of sacramentalism that denies the truth and reality that "faith comes by hearing."[1] The sacramentality of preaching and preaching's iconic nature is maintained only so far as both Word and Sacrament are held in symbiotic relationship — as long as the pulpit keeps sight of the altar, and as the altar looks back to the pulpit — so far as preaching Christ crucified is situated between both font and altar.

Since Orthodox preaching is sacramental by virtue of its symbiotic relationship with the Holy Mysteries in a liturgical setting, the sermon emerges as incarnational. "As a sacramental, preaching is not just a priest speaking. It is a divine-human encounter. It is God continuing to reveal himself in Christ, seeking the lost, healing the broken, lifting the fallen, bringing the dead to life. It is God in Christ calling all to join him in loving toil for the kingdom."[2] In the words of Hopko, "Preaching God's Word is a sacramental act, an essential element in the liturgical action of God the Father, the Lord Jesus Christ and the Holy Spirit. When the bishop or priest stands to deliver the liturgical sermon, it is truly 'time for the Lord to act.'"[3] Within the Orthodox theological

---

1   Rom. 10:17, NKJV.

2   Coniaris, 7.

3   Hopko, 176.

tradition, this incarnational aspect of the ministry of the Word has its basis in the *synergeia* between God's divine initiative and the human response of the priest and the people. Joseph Allen elaborates:

> ...one can see, from the Old Testament through our own time, this ministry of the word is realized through a true Divine-human dynamic: God, as "the One Shepherd," has given these words as gifts to us, that through our "struggle" with them (and in truth, through our sweat and effort to transform them) we may give them distinct and human form, thereby transmitting them to others (Ecc 12:11). In this way rhetoric as the "right word," with the true, ultimate and final meaning of those words, is realized through human cooperation with God himself, who lifts this process up and gives it its efficacy. Together, they offer to the world the way to faith and true life.[1]

In the frailty and brokenness of our own humanity, God has ordained that we become bearers of the precious gift of the Gospel; and in that actuality, we realize that we "have this treasure in earthen vessels."[2] In this synergistic relationship of the human and

---

1 Joseph J. Allen, *The Ministry of the Church: The Image of Pastoral Care* (Crestwood, New York: St. Vladimir's Seminary Press, 1986), 138.

2 2 Cor. 4:7, RSV.

the divine, the Gospel truly becomes the Word of God when given voice by the human preacher. "As a messenger, he delivers the word; as a witness, he bears testimony that the word is divine. He reveals God, makes an invisible God audible. Not by proving or arguing. His words are charged with divine power."[1] In his classic work, *A Faith to Proclaim*, theologian James Stewart also affirms the incarnational reality of preaching:

> The Gospel existed and lived, not in documentary evidence and doctrinal formulae, but only in being proclaimed....just as the corporate life of the Church was Christ's daily renewed self-disclosure in the power of His Resurrection, so the preaching of the word was in actual fact the living personal Word breaking in from the beyond, taking charge of the situation and going creatively to work.[2]

The preacher, within the midst of the assembly, gives voice to the Gospel, and through the power of the Holy Spirit transforms the material signs (*signum*) of words and text into the reality (*res*) of what is proclaimed.

---

1   Walter J. Burghardt, *Preaching: The Art and Craft* (Mahwah, New Jersey: Paulist Press, 1987), 33.

2   James S. Stewart, *A Faith to Proclaim* (Vancouver, British Columbia: Regent College Publishing, 1953), 43.

The task of the minister of today…is to bring the written Word to living speech. The Word of God written is not the same thing as the Word of God preached. That is why in both the synagogue and the church the Word is read as well as preached.… It is the job of the preacher to make the Word of God, the Word the prophets put into writing, a living reality for the congregation.[1]

Finally, as proffered by Townshend, "This work [preaching] is done by human language. However, it only takes effect, and comes alive, through the Word and Spirit of God."[2]

Clearly, the sacramentality of preaching is integral to the divine work of God in mediating His grace and holy presence through the material signs of both Word and Sacrament. Therefore the appropriate place for preaching as the oral icon of Christ is in the midst of the liturgical assembly where God has chosen to reveal Himself through the weakness of human words and through the common elements of bread and wine. The Gospel may certainly be proclaimed by the evangelist in a stadium or on the street corner, but preaching that is truly iconic is preaching that is united to the worship of God in the fullness of sacramental grace. Archimandrite Zacharias states, "In the Liturgy we

---

1 Old, *The Biblical Period*, 58–9.

2 Townshend, 62.

embrace the past and the future and refer all things back to God in full and all-embracing thanksgiving for all those things which God has done for us in order to set us before His face."[1] It is therefore within the context of the Divine Liturgy, in the Eternal Now of God, that Orthodox preaching finds its proper place; that the iconic nature of preaching as a facet of God's self-revelation is made fully manifest. For above all things, it is in the Liturgy where we will indeed discover and affirm that *Christ is in our midst.*

---

[1] Archimandrite Zacharias, *The Enlargement of the Heart*, ed. Christopher Veniamin (Dalton, PA: Mount Thabor Publishing, 2012), 103–4.

Chapter 3

PRESENTING THE ICON:
THE REVELATORY ART OF PREACHING

> Human beings are not converted by
> having truths about Jesus presented
> to them but by having Jesus Himself
> presented to them. Without realizing
> what they are doing our contemporaries
> are asking the Church for what long
> ago some Greeks asked the apostles:
> "We want to see Jesus"....
> — Raniero Cantalamessa,
> *The Mystery of God's Word*

With the oral icon of Christ prepared and properly
placed in the context of liturgical worship, the act of
preaching becomes the means by which the icon is
presented to the listeners — it is through the revelatory
art of preaching whereby the Risen Lord is made present
in the assembly. Orthodox preaching is not simply a

discipline of faithfully and accurately communicating the propositional truths of the Gospel (though that remains foundational), but is largely a divinely inspired art of creating word images that are appropriated by the listeners in order to personally and intimately encounter the radical demands of the Gospel in the midst of the holy, transforming, life-giving, healing presence of the Lord Himself. The revelatory art of preaching, therefore, is not solely a human endeavor, but neither is the human quality of preaching swallowed up in the divine, as Florovsky explains, "There is no accommodation to human frailty. The point is rather that the human tongue does not lose its natural features to become a vehicle of divine revelation. If we want the divine word to ring clear, our tongue is not to leave off being human. What is human is not swept away by divine inspiration, it is only *transfigured*. The 'supernatural' does not destroy what is 'natural'...."[1] Iconic preaching, then, as a synergistic divine-human endeavor becomes an artistic work transfigured by the power of the Divine. Clark notes, "By presenting the story of salvation through the medium of the arts, liturgical celebration aids in engaging additional creative aspects of the human psyche, serving both to amplify the challenging message presented by the liturgical texts and to facilitate its assimilation by those gathered to participate."[2] While

---

1   Florovsky, 27.

2   Clark, 36–7.

we have already examined the sacramental nature of preaching within the context of the Liturgy, we now want to focus upon those qualities of preaching which lends to its artistic nature; that is, to consider the means by which preaching at its best is truly iconic and thereby mediates the presence of Christ.

Not every artistic style of preaching is effective in every age. In the patristic age of the Church when classical rhetoric reigned supreme, the iconic nature of Orthodox preaching was largely mediated by the eloquence of style in such formal and elaborate oratory which was anticipated by the listener. The homilies of Saint John Chrysostom exist as the most prolific examples of the employment of classical rhetoric in preaching. Such a style, however, would be largely lost on today's typical postmodern listener. And yet, as we shall see, there is something about these classical sermons of St. John Chrysostom which remains fundamentally iconic to this day. So while artistic style may vary greatly in Orthodox preaching across the ages and cultures, we must recognize that it is not a particular sermonic style which determines the iconic nature of preaching. Rather it is the preacher's ability (through divine assistance) in utilizing the vernacular of the day to effectively craft powerful, efficacious word images for the listeners to receive. Language and style is always time and culture conditioned, but the listener's ability to appropriate truth through effectively created word pictures abides as a universal. It is from this premise that we will examine the inductive approach to preaching as most fitting with the essence and goal of iconic preaching.

Inductive preaching is distinguished from a deductive approach in that it proceeds from a place of experience and the "how" rather than by the logical rationalism of deduction and the "why." Craddock further explains, "There are basically two directions in which thought moves: deductive and inductive. Simply stated, deductive movement is from the general truth to the particular application or experience, while induction is the reverse."[1] Inductive preaching is naturally more effective than a deductive approach, particularly in our postmodern age since, as Craddock argues, it conforms to how we experience life:

> Everyone lives inductively, not deductively. No farmer deals with the problem of calfhood, only with the calf. The woman in the kitchen is not occupied with the culinary arts in general but with a particular roast or cake. The wood craftsman is hardly able to discuss intelligently the topic of "chairness," but is a master with a chair. We will speak of the sun rising and setting long after everyone knows better. The minister says "All people are mortal" and meets drowsy agreement;

---

1 Fred B. Craddock, *As One Without Authority* (St. Louis, Missouri: Chalice Press, 2001), 45.

he announces that "Mr. Brown's son is dying," and the church becomes the church.[1]

In fact, Craddock goes so far as to say that "the incarnation itself is the inductive method. From experiences with the man Jesus of Nazareth, conclusions about God were reached, usually after painful revision."[2] Haddon Robinson also affirms the essential value of inductive preaching, particularly in our current society:

Inductive sermons have special appeal to inhabitants of a culture dominated by television and motion pictures. We have become a storied culture. Whether it is a mystery drama, a comedy, or even a sports contest, there is a large element of induction. The drama isn't solved until the end of the last act, and the joke leads up to the punch line, and the sports event moves toward the final score. Inductive sermons fit that way of thinking....You connect with a modern audience when you tell a biblical story with insight and imagination.[3]

Since iconic preaching is all about presenting the listeners with word images of the Gospel rather

---

[1] Ibid., 51.

[2] Ibid., 52.

[3] Haddon Robinson, *Biblical Preaching*, Second Edition (Grand Rapids, Michigan: Baker Academic, 2001), 129.

than bare propositional truth, it only follows that an inductive approach to preaching abides as the most effective means of reaching the listener. John Piper argues, "Experience and Scripture teach that the heart is most powerfully touched not when the mind is entertaining abstract ideas, but when it is filled with vivid images of amazing reality."[1]

The inductive approach, when utilized iconically in preaching, may be compared with the use of inverse perspective in Byzantine icons. As Leonid Ouspensky asserts, "The preservation of the reality of the plane is greatly assisted by so-called inverse perspective, the point of departure of which lies not in the depth of the image, but in front of the image, as it were in the spectator himself."[2] Like the utilization of inverse perspective in iconography, inductive preaching invites the listener into a living encounter with the truth of the Gospel. By induction, the listener is not simply a passive recipient of propositions, but becomes an active participant in salvation history by engaging the truth of the Gospel at a personal and subjective level. It is at this level that he may consequently appropriate the Gospel as his own.

---

1 John Piper, *The Supremacy of God in Preaching* (Grand Rapids, MI: Baker Books, 2004), 90.

2 Ouspensky, Leonid, and Vladimir Lossky, *The Meaning of Icons*, trans. G.E.H. Palmer, & E. Kadloubovsky (Crestwood, New York: St. Vladimir's Seminary Press, 1982), 41.

The archetypal model for inductive preaching is the parabolic preaching of Jesus. Craddock indicates that the parable "lies at the heart of Jesus' preaching. Here the whole of life is concentrated into one concrete situation. Jesus does not make a call for faith in general but in relation to a specific life situation. The subject matter is not the nature of God but the hearer's situation in the light of God."[1] Similarly, Coniaris notes, "Jesus joined sight and sound, the ear and the eye, through his extensive use of parables. He turned on the lights, illuminated his sermons with numerous illustrations. He painted beautiful pictures with words so that people could not only hear, but also see the truth."[2] Clearly, it is the parabolic preaching of Jesus that serves as the preacher's supreme example of how he may engage the hearts and minds of the listeners. DeBona states, "The inductive sermon organized around narrative logic reaches out and grabs the congregation, compelling them into the "how" of Christian existence, a question posed by the scriptures themselves, especially evident in the parables of Jesus."[3]

Effective preaching today may certainly not replicate the exact genre or literary style of Jesus' teachings in a technical sense, but preaching within

---

1 Craddock, *As One Without Authority*, 50.

2 Coniaris, 84.

3 DeBona, 30.

our time must nonetheless follow the same general inductive and parabolic form. Old argues how this form is extracted from our own life experiences:

> Preaching in its very nature is parabolic, just as life in its very nature is parabolic. Life is filled with signs and intimations of a higher unseen reality. The sowing of seed, its growth, fruition, and harvest is one of those signs, as is the beauty of a pearl. The sharing of a meal is a powerful sign. The relation of sheep to a shepherd, the relation between mother and child, the marriage relationship, and by all means the marriage feast — all are signs of the fundamental realities of existence. They are not only fundamental but ultimate realities.[1]

Whether it was a sermon preached in Constantinople 1,600 years ago, or a homily given in Baltimore last Sunday, the preacher's ability to present the Gospel as an oral icon of Christ and in a manner that effectively engages the listeners is largely dependent upon his ability to artistically and imaginatively employ the use of symbols and word images. Constantine Scouteris affirms that the "use of symbols, icons, parables and metaphors is fundamental to the scriptural approach to divine revelation. It is the language of the prophets, the 'teaching method'

---

1 Old, *The Biblical Period*, 145.

of our Lord, God and Saviour Jesus Christ, and the foundation of the apostolic interpretation of Christ, his mission and the Church."[1] Orthodox preaching therefore can do no less, especially as it functions as an important aspect of God's self-revelation.

We now turn to specific and concrete examples of iconic preaching from two different churchmen on two different continents in order to consider the specific aspects of their preaching which conformed to the inductive approach of Jesus' teaching and preaching. We first want to examine the preaching of St. John Chrysostom (c. 347–407) in the Byzantine East, and in turn consider the preaching of St. Peter Chrysologus (380–c. 450) in the Latin West. As we will examine, the preaching of these two saints represents a diversity of cultural and linguistic styles which connected with the people of their time and place. It was *not* the outward style, the language, or the historical context which rendered their preaching as iconic, but rather their skill in artistically crafting word images, all toward the inductive method of presenting Jesus as "visible" to their listeners and thereby inducing holy imitation within their hearts.

The repertoire of St. John Chrysostom's extant homilies represents such an extensive expanse of diverse theological and homiletical subject matters

---

1   Constantine B. Scouteris, *Ecclesial Being: Contributions to the Theological Dialogue*, ed. Christopher Veniamin (South Canaan, PA: Mount Thabor Publishing, 2005), 110–1.

that only a minute sampling is appropriate for the scope of this study. Specifically, we will consider two excerpts from Chrysostom's preaching on Pauline texts whereby the master homiletical artist crafts portraitures of the beloved Apostle Paul. The iconic nature of these homilies derives from an inductive method of preaching, as evidenced by these fine excerpts. The first example is from Chrysostom's *Homily 13* on 1 Corinthians 4:16:

Let us see then in what way he [Paul] followed Christ: for this imitation needs not time and art, but a steady purpose alone. Thus if we go into the study of a painter, we shall not be able to copy the portrait, though we see it ten thousand times. But to copy him we are enabled by hearing alone. Will ye then that we bring the tablet before you and sketch out for you Paul's manner of life? Well, let it be produced, that picture far brighter than all the images of Emperors: for its material is not boards glued together, nor canvass stretched out; but the material is the work of God: being as it is a soul and a body: a soul, the work of God, not of men; and a body again in like wise...

...And first he shows the head of the king, preaching Christ; then also the remainder of the body; the body of a perfect Christian life. Now painters we know shut themselves up and execute all their works with great nicety and in quiet; not opening the doors to any one: but this man, setting forth his tablet in the view of the world, in the midst of universal opposition, clamor, disturbance, did under such circumstances work out this Royal Image, and was not hindered. And therefore he said, We are made a spectacle unto the world; in the midst of earth, and sea, and the heaven, and the whole habitable globe, and the world both material and intellectual, he was drawing that portrait of his.

Would you like to see the other parts also thereof from the head downwards? Or will you that from below we carry our description upwards? Contemplate then a statue of gold or rather of something more costly than gold, and such as might stand in heaven; not fixed with lead nor placed in one spot, but hurrying from Jerusalem even unto Illyricum, Romans 15:19 and setting forth into Spain, and borne as it were on wings over every part of the world. For what could be more beautiful than these feet which visited the whole earth under the sun? This same beauty the prophet also from of old proclaims, saying, (Isaiah 52:7) "How beautiful are the feet of them that preach the Gospel of peace!" Have you seen how fair are the feet? Will you see the bosom too? Come, let me show you this also, and you shall behold it far more splendid than these beautiful, yea even than the bosom itself of the ancient lawgiver. For Moses indeed carried tablets of stone: but this man within him had Christ Himself: it was the very image of the King which he bore.[1]

In her seminal work, *The Heavenly Trumpet*, Margaret Mitchell exhaustively analyzes the Pauline interpretation of John Chrysostom as revealed through his homiletical epithets of St. Paul. Mitchell reveals how Chrysostom, employing a type of *ekphrasis*,[2] created these portraitures of the beloved Apostle Paul for one principal reason:

---

1 John Chrysostom, *Nicene and Post-Nicene Fathers: Chrysostom: Homilies on First and Second Corinthians*, ed. Philip Schaff, Vol. 12 (Peabody, Massachusetts: Hendrickson Publishers, Inc., 1999), 74–5.

2 Mitchell indicates that *ekphrasis* (ἐκφρασις) was "an ancient rhetorical form that was designed expressly to merge the literary and graphic arts, and create with words a vivid, lifelike encounter between an audience and a person or work of art they were unable to see." This literary method was intended to overcome the challenge of the listeners in receiving a message through hearing alone. "The preacher in interpreting the Scriptures formulates a powerful image and then represents that portrait in such vivid terms that all will as much as 'see' it and its brilliance which rivals the imperial portraits." Margaret M. Mitchell, *The Heavenly Trumpet: John Chrysostom and the Art of Pauline Interpretation* (Louisville, Kentucky: Westminster John Knox Press, 2002), 41–53ff.

...to render the apostolic form visible and memorable so that it could be imitated by the next generations of hearers, who would have access to Paul through lovingly engaging his soul as engraved in his monuments, the letters. Via his reading of resuscitation, in which he heard the voice of Paul and then extended it to others by composing portraits of the author in his exposition of letters he wrote, Chrysostom midwifed a living conversation and relationship between the dead Paul and the living Christian congregation.[1]

Chrysostom crafted these vivid images of Paul in more than just one homily so that the faithful would be confronted repeatedly with an explicit oral icon of the beloved Apostle. Another example of one of these portraitures is taken from Chrysostom's *Homily 32* on Romans 16:17, 18:

Fain would I see the dust of those eyes which were blinded gloriously, which recovered their sight again for the salvation of the world; which even in the body were counted worthy to see Christ, which saw earthly things, yet saw them not, which saw the things which are not seen, which saw not sleep, which were watchful at midnight, which were not effected as eyes are. I would also

---

1   Mitchell, 65.

see the dust of those feet, which ran through the world and were not weary; which were bound in the stocks when the prison shook, which went through parts habitable or uninhabited, which walked on so many journeys. And why need I speak of single parts? Fain would I see the tomb, where the armor of righteousness is laid up, the armor of light, the limbs which now live, but which in life were made dead; and in all whereof Christ lived, which were crucified to the world, which were Christ's members, which were clad in Christ, were a temple of the Spirit, an holy building, bound in the Spirit…riveted to the fear of God, which had the marks of Christ.

…Let us then, laying all this to heart, stand nobly; for Paul was a man, partaking of the same nature with us, and having everything else in common with us. But because he showed such great love toward Christ, he went up above the Heavens, and stood with the Angels. And so if we too would rouse ourselves up some little, and kindle in ourselves that fire, we shall be able to emulate that holy man.[1]

1　John Chrysostom, *Nicene and Post-Nicene Fathers: Chrysostom: Homilies on the Acts of the Apostles and Epistle to the Romans*, ed. Philip Schaff. Vol. 11, (Peabody, Massachusetts: Hendrickson Publishers, Inc., 1999), 563–4.

These masterfully crafted homiletical epithets of Paul illustrate Chrysostom's ability to create powerful word images with the explicit intention of motivating his listeners toward holy imitation of the Apostle, who as Chrysostom affirmed, served as an icon of Christ. Theodor Nikolaou asserts, "The didactic goal is thus achieved by both the story-teller and the painter, in that both recall an event and thus stimulate the onlooker or listener to imitation…."[1] To imitate St. Paul in all of his virtue and glory was to indeed imitate Christ.[2] Allen indicates, "Christ is revealed in St Paul, and then Paul preaches out of the very person of Christ. He first 'receives' this ministry of the word which is delivered to him, and then he delivers it to others."[3] Without question, Chrysostom who had received this ministry was faithful in presenting St. Paul in these Pauline homilies, and in so doing, he was presenting Christ. The power of Chrysostom's preaching lay in the iconic nature of his preaching — the infusing of vivid word pictures with the inductive method of allowing the listeners to appropriate for themselves the virtuous example of St. Paul and the subsequent desire for holy imitation.

Even outside of the purview of Pauline preaching and the associated Pauline portraitures, Chrysostom

---

1 Nikolaou, 324.

2 Mitchell, 396.

3 Allen, 131.

established himself as a master in the homiletic arts of creating powerful and colorful word pictures through the employment of metaphorical language and literary devices. As with his Pauline preaching, these homilies engaged the listeners with graphic word images which captured their attention and ultimately presented to them the oral icon of Christ. Within Orthodoxy, Chrysostom's *Paschal Homily* abides as the most popular and perhaps most excellent example of such iconic preaching:

> He that was taken by death has annihilated it! He descended into hades and took hades captive! He embittered it when it tasted his flesh! And anticipating this Isaiah exclaimed, "Hades was embittered when it encountered thee in the lower regions." It was embittered, for it was abolished! It was embittered, for it was mocked! It was embittered, for it was purged! It was embittered, for it was despoiled! It was embittered, for it was bound in chains!

> It took a body and, face to face, met God! It took earth and encountered heaven! It took what it saw but crumbled before what it had not seen!

> "O death, where is thy sting? O hades, where is thy victory?"
> Christ is risen, and you are overthrown!

Christ is risen, and the demons are fallen!
Christ is risen, and the angels rejoice!
Christ is risen, and life reigns!
Christ is risen, and not one dead remains in a tomb!

For Christ, being raised from the dead, has become the First-fruits of them that slept.

To him be glory and might unto ages of ages. Amen.[1]

Chrysostom's personification of death and Hades, his evocative language (e.g., "tasted his flesh," "abolished," "purged," "bound in chains"), and the masterful and poetic utilization of parallelism and imagery all contribute to the highly iconic nature of this classical homily. In essence, Chrysostom succeeded in creating and presenting to the listeners a powerful oral image of the Risen Christ. Completely absent is any sort of philological or deductive argumentation. This homily rather represents a glorious example of inductive preaching whereby the people are presented with the image of Truth which they may appropriate as their own — the homily becomes the means for a personal and intimate holy encounter with the Risen Lord; an encounter which calls for a doxological response.

---

[1] John Chrysostom, "Paschal Homily," *Orthodox Wiki*, http://orthodoxwiki.org/Paschal_Homily (accessed June 30, 2013).

As Chrysostom was esteemed as the "Golden Mouth" in the East, his contemporary in the Latin West, Peter Chrysologus, was distinguishing himself as the "Golden-Worded." Considerably less rhetorical than Chrysostom, Chrysologus' idiom tended toward a less formal and more direct style. His homiletical craft, however, was no less iconic and creative than Chrysostom's. Chrysologus' utilization of illustrations and descriptive language followed the example of Jesus' parabolic preaching, and to this day are highly readable homilies. The following are a few select excerpts from the homilies of Peter Chrysologus, the Bishop of Ravenna:

Sermon 114, "Slaves to the Law and to Grace"
A traveler always finds it sweet and pleasant to return to his own home. The courtyards of his ancestral home are attractive to him after an absence. Similarly, after these intervals, I find it sweeter to return to my series of passages from the Apostle [Paul]. Some necessity of religion often compels us to depart from the order of discourses which we had intended, and from the straight path which our discourse was to follow. For, we must so control the sequence of our instruction that one matter does not hinder another. Wherefore, let us hear what the holy Apostle has told us today....[1]

---

1 Peter Chrysologus, *The Fathers of the Church: Saint Peter*

Sermon 106: "On the Fig To Be Chopped Down"

Just as a skillful teacher strikes at the intellects of students who are inexperienced in listening and slow to understand by employing various teaching techniques, and arouses and enkindles their talents, so does the Lord with a variety of parables and diverse metaphors call together and invite the sluggish and slow minds of the peoples to listen to the Gospel. For indeed the Lord begins today as follows: *A certain person had a fig tree planted in his vineyard, and he came to look for fruit on it, and did not find any. So he said to his vinedresser: "Look, it has been three years now since I have been coming to look for fruit on this fig tree, and still I have found none. Cut it down; for why does it take up space on the land?" But he said in response: "Lord, let it be for this year, until I dig around it and apply manure, and see if it bears fruit, but if not you can cut it down then"* (Lk 13. 6–9).[1]

Sermon 8: "On the Lenten Fast"

When a prudent captain casts off from the coast,

Chrysologus, Selected Sermons and Saint Valerian Homilies, ed. Roy Joseph Deferrari, trans. George E. Ganss, Vol. 17 (New York: Fathers of the Church, Inc., 1953), 184–5.

1 Peter Chrysologus, *The Fathers of the Church, St. Peter Chrysologus, Selected Sermons, Volume 3*, ed. Thomas P. Halton, trans. William B. Palardy, Vol. 110 (Washington, DC: The Catholic University of America Press, 2005), 137.

when he enters the deep to journey across the sea, he puts aside his concerns for his home, his country, his wife, his children; and he is totally consumed in mind, body, and emotion with the tasks of sailing that he is able overcome the perilous waves and, victorious over danger, enters the quarters of a profitable port. So we too, my brothers, having set out along the route of abstinence, on the sea of fasting, on the journey of Lent, let us cast the ship of our body off from the coast of the world, let us renounce our concerns for our earthly country, let us fully unfurl the sails of our mind on the mast of the cross; let us secure the safe passage of our vessel with the ropes of the virtues, with the oars of wisdom, with the rudders of discipline; and having set forth from the land let us gaze upon the sky, so that by the guidance of the signs of heaven along the clear and narrow paths of our hidden journey we might hold our course unobstructed. And so with Christ as our pilot and the Holy Spirit providing the wind, when the foam of the pleasures has been overcome, the waves of the vices have been conquered, the storms of the misdeeds weathered, the rocks of sin evaded, and when we have steered clear of the vessels of all the offenses, then let us enter the port of Easter, life's reward, the joys of the resurrection.[1]

---

1 Peter Chrysologus, *The Fathers of the Church: St. Peter Chryso-*

These brief sermon excerpts serve to illustrate Chrysologus' homiletical art and skill in crafting descriptive word images which inductively convey the Gospel in a manner that is accessible to his listeners, and by which the people may interpret their own lives in the light of the Gospel. While Chrysologus does not employ the same rhetorical style and flair as his Byzantine contemporary, his imaginative use of illustrations, similes, and metaphors (especially as embodied the last example, Sermon 8, "On the Lenten Fast") nonetheless renders his preaching just as powerful and iconic. Like Chrysostom, Chrysologus imaginatively and creatively crafts the spoken word to present oral icons of Truth to his listeners — icons which they encounter and ultimately discern (with divine assistance) as the Risen Christ in their midst.

Both Chrysostom and Chrysologus represent the "gold standard" of classical iconic Orthodox preaching. Though contemporaries, their contrasting literary styles situated in two different cultures demonstrate how diversified preaching may actually be while retaining the essence and marks of superior iconic preaching in Orthodoxy. It serves to support the premise that regardless of the culture or the historical period, the essence of iconic Orthodox

logus, *Selected Sermons, Volume 2*, ed. Thomas P. Halton, trans. William B. Palardy, Vol. 109 (Washington, DC: The Catholic University of America Press, 2004), 42–3.

preaching remains universal and unchanged. This means that even in our relativistic postmodern culture, Orthodox preaching has the ability to break into the lives of people if the preacher skillfully, artfully, and imaginatively presents word images as the means of inductively moving the listeners from particular truth grounded in experience to the objective truth of the Gospel which they are able to appropriate as their own. "We cannot raise a dead daughter to life; our words will not stop inflation or lower unemployment. What our words can do is help people make connections between the realities of their lives and the realities of the Gospel."[1] In the presentation of the oral icon of Christ through preaching, the interpretative task shifts from the preacher and his interpretation of Scripture to the listener and his interpretation of his own life and concrete circumstances in light of the Gospel.

Critical to the revelatory art of iconic preaching is the preacher's ability to craft effective word images whereby the listener's imagination is redeemed and transformed by the truth of the Gospel. Craddock explains:

Description provides images, and images are necessary for removing from the mind inadequate, erroneous, distorted attitudes and behavior. Along

---

1 United States Conference of Catholic Bishops, 10.

the hallways of the mind hang images, fixed and influential, hung there by experience, education, associations, stories heard or read, and by countless forces more subtle but no less effective….Images must be replaced, and this comes only gradually, by other images. In the ministry of preaching, much of this burden falls on description. In other words, we are not discussing how to decorate a sermon, but how to preach.[1]

Iconic Orthodox preaching is the appropriate prescription for replacing these worldly images and icons within the soul. Burghardt asserts that, "…our task [as preachers] is to shatter false images, to destroy idols."[2] Toward that end, the preacher, through the effective and judicious use of illustrations, metaphors, similes, parables, and other descriptive language and literary devices (e.g., imagery, alliteration, parallelisms, juxtapositions, etc.), is able to present vivid icons of Truth. As Coniaris indicates, "The preacher's function is to turn the ear into an eye so that what is heard may also be seen. The preacher is called to be an artist painting pictures with words. In the words of Halford Luccock we need 'to give our message a sight track, as well as a sound track.'"[3]

---

1 Craddock, *Preaching*, 201.

2 Burghardt, 35.

3 Coniaris, 83–4.

In the last analysis, iconic preaching is not about delighting or entertaining — it is *not* about the preacher and his own egotistical needs, but is rather about bringing the faithful into a holy encounter with Christ. As indicated by Piper, "Preaching that does not have the aroma of God's greatness may entertain for a season, but it will not touch the hidden cry of the soul: 'Show me thy glory!'"[1] It is the revelation of that divine glory through superior Orthodox preaching artfully presented that touches the deepest need of the human soul; that provides the vehicle for bringing us to a place of repentance and moving us ever toward union with God. For the mark of a truly effective sermon is not in the degree the listeners were emotionally stirred or intellectually stimulated, but rather in how effective it was in bringing the listeners face to face with Jesus.[2] By following the example of our Lord in His parabolic preaching, and in modeling the homiletical craft of great Orthodox preachers within our own vernacular and cultural milieu, we have the opportunity to present to the faithful a wonderful gift of Christ's presence. It is Orthodox preaching, when artfully and imaginatively crafted, and inductively presented by the preacher through the inspiration of the Holy Spirit, which manifests

---

1 Piper, 13.

2 Coniaris, 18.

as the oral icon of Christ, and enables the faithful to encounter for themselves the presence of the Lord and the transforming power of His Word.

Chapter 4

ENGAGING THE ICON:
THE ROLE OF PREACHING
IN ORTHODOX SPIRITUALITY

> Thus the human being is not created for
> autonomous and self-sufficient life, but
> rather for participation in divine life; it
> is only "in God" that he can realize his
> original destination. Nothing is more
> "natural" for man than to live and grow
> in grace.
> — Nicholas Ozoline,
> *"The Theology of the Icon"*

In Chapter 3 we examined the revelatory art of
preaching as the presentation of the oral icon of
Christ whereby the presence of our Lord is mediated
and made manifest. Such a holy encounter however
demands a response. It is not enough to simply
present the oral icon of Christ and for the listener to
passively receive it, regardless of how effective that

presentation may be and how attentive the listener may remain. It is also not enough to simply assent to the propositional truths of the Word of God. With the iconic and prophetic proclamation of the Gospel, one must subsequently engage the oral icon. That is, even as the listener is humbled and repentant in response to hearing the Gospel proclaimed, he must pass through the doorway of transcendence which is opened up through a supernatural encounter with the Risen Christ mediated sacramentally through the iconically and prophetically preached Gospel within the context of the Divine Liturgy. In this final chapter we will consider the ultimate end (*telos*) of preaching and its role in Orthodox spirituality. We will examine the doxological and anagogical aspect of preaching that mystically transports the assembly beyond the sign and symbol of the spoken Word and into the transcendent, contemplative vision of God where true repentance may be affected and the healing of the fractured soul may occur. It is this transcendent aspect of preaching which derives from God and at once takes us to God where true reform and amendment of heart and life takes place, as noted by Yves Congar, "God's plan, as the Bible reveals it to us, can be considered as a process that moves from outside to inside, from symbols accessible to the senses toward another reality that changes the very person."[1]

---

1   Yves M J Congar, "'Real' Liturgy, 'Real' Preaching," *Worship* 82,

In the end, it is the oral icon of Christ which abides as a principal means of opening up the transcendent realm of the Divine in which we move toward *theosis* (divinization), and by which we ourselves as children of grace may become icons of God.

In examining the role of preaching in Orthodox spirituality, we must first consider the prophetic dimension of the proclamation of the Gospel. As Saint Paul indicates, "And his gifts were that some should be apostles, some prophets, some evangelists, some pastors and teachers...."[1] The bishop, priest, or deacon functioning *as prophet* is most explicitly manifest in his preaching of the Good News of Jesus Christ. Saint Paul understood the personal and sacred responsibility for faithfully and prophetically proclaiming the Gospel when he wrote, "For necessity is laid upon me. Woe to me if I do not preach the gospel!"[2] To neglect the sacred vocation of preaching or to water down the message of the Gospel is to disregard and to abdicate the prophetic witness of the Church in calling all people to repentance and salvation. Conversely, to diligently and faithfully proclaim the Gospel of Christ is to actualize the living nature of the Church, as indicated by Bobrinskoy, "...the Church's prophetic ministry is

---

no. 4 (2008): 311.

[1] Eph. 4:11, RSV.

[2] 1 Cor. 9:16, RSV.

not merely doctrine, it is a living doctrine, a witness to the living truth of Christ, an inner learning, a begetting of new sons in the Spirit, and missionary preaching in the folly of the Cross and the scandal of the gospel."[1] The prophetic ministry of the Church as realized in the faithful preaching of Her clergy is therefore foundational to Orthodox spirituality, especially as the Gospel is proclaimed iconically and with the intent of bringing the listeners to a place of repentance, healing, and salvation.

In acknowledging the prophetic dimension of preaching we must next consider how the artistic aspect of iconic preaching functions toward its spiritual end. Language which is rooted in an aspect of covenant (i.e., a people of common tongue agreeing on the meaning of words) possesses a sacramental nature, in that language is comprised of signs and symbols of a greater transcendent reality (the *res* or essence/reality of the signs). When language is utilized artistically, it moves the listener from the grammatical and literal meaning of words toward the invisible realm of transcendence. Language that is employed iconically (in contrast to a mere artistic form) functions incarnationally by making visible the invisible in the very signs and symbols of language such that God Himself is revealed:

---

1 Boris Bobrinskoy, *The Mystery of the Church: A Course in Orthodox Dogmatic Theology*, trans. Michael Breck (Yonkers, New York: St. Vladimir's Seminary Press, 2012), 174.

Fine art reveals the worldly, orienting the eye to the spiritual search for the invisible. Religious iconography is the converse — it reveals the invisible Spirit, oriented toward the world so as to become incarnate within material, symbolic images. Iconography leads artists out of the images of blurry suppositions and fickle opinions and brings them to the contemplation of the unified image of God within our own souls, manifesting this soul as a living mirror of the glory of God. Iconography does not search for formal answers to questions about truth; it *depicts* the Truth within the forms of God's presence appropriate for contemplation.[1]

So the artistry of language, particularly as it is utilized iconically and incarnationally, serves as a medium for making manifest and visible the invisible and transcendent realities of the Divine. Burghardt asserts that the "homily is a fascinating wedding of all those ways in which imagination comes to expression: vision and ritual, symbol and story (parable, allegory, and myth), the fine arts. This is the homily at its best, the homily that makes God's wonderful works come alive, immerses in the mystery, evokes a religious response."[2] From this we can begin to understand how the artistic use of language employed in iconic

---

1 Andrejev, 63.

2 Burghardt, 23.

preaching can serve to mediate the presence of the Lord and to lead the listener into the spiritual realm of transcendence.

Poetry which is often called "the language of the heart" is perhaps the most effective linguistic medium by which one is transported beyond the literal meaning of the words to the greater transcendent reality conveyed by the language. The ambiguity of poetic language in concert with its highly expressive idiom forces the listener away from the surface meaning and into the realm of imagination. However, when poetry is employed iconically (from an Orthodox perspective), the listener is not left to his own imagination and flights of fantasy, but is rather guided into the very realm of divine transcendence; for in finding the door of his heart, he "will discover it is the door of the kingdom of God."[1] Poetry therefore becomes a particularly powerful medium when it is employed in Orthodox preaching. The Syrian Fathers were renowned for the crafting of homiletical hymns — poetic sermons which were intrinsically mystical and that served to carry the listeners into the place of doxological transcendence. Perhaps the greatest of these preaching poets was St. Ephraim the Syrian. His poetic craft is exemplified in his *Homiletical Hymn #1 on the Nativity*:

---

[1] John Chrysostom, as quoted by Anthony Bloom, *Beginning to Pray* (Mahwah, NJ: Paulist Press, 1970), 46.

In this night of reconcilement let no man be wroth or gloomy!
In this night that stills all, none that threatens or disturbs!
This night belongs to the sweet One; bitter or harsh be in it none!
In this night that is the meek One's, high or haughty be in it none!

In this day of pardoning let us not exact trespasses!
In this day of gladnesses let us not spread sadnesses!
In this day so sweet, let us not be harsh!
In this day of peaceful rest, let us not be wrathful in it!

In this day when God came to sinners,
Let not the righteous be in his mind uplifted over sinner!
In this day in which there came the Lord of all unto the servants,
Let masters too condescend to their servants lovingly!

In this day in which the Rich became poor for our sakes,
Let the rich man make the poor man share with him at his table.

On this day to us came forth the Gift, although we asked it not!

Let us therefore bestow alms on them that cry and beg of us.

This is the day that opened for us a gate on high to our prayers.

Let us open also gates to supplicants that have transgressed, and of us have asked [forgiveness.]

To-day the Lord of nature was against His nature changed;

Let it not to us be irksome to turn our evil wills.

Fixed in nature is the body; great or less it cannot become:

But the will has such dominion, it can grow to any measure.

To-day Godhead sealed itself upon Manhood,

That so with the Godhead's stamp Manhood might be adorned.[1]

Old notes that the "whole purpose of poetry is to intimate more than is said, and it is quite clear that Ephrem understands very well that this is what needs to be done when one is talking about a subject like this. Poetry must always have a certain reserve, one

---

[1] Ephraim the Syrian, *Nicene and Post-Nicene Fathers*, ed. Philip Schaff, & Henry Wace, trans. J. B. Morris, Vol. 13 (Peabody, Massachusetts: Hendrickson Publishers, Inc., 1999), 226.

might almost say, a certain modesty."[1] The linguistic skill of St. Ephraim in the above example not only proclaims the propositional truth of the Nativity for the listener to affirm, but Ephraim's poetic preaching brings truth from the cognitive level of the head into the spiritual realm of the heart; from a mere historical fact perceived and affirmed to an internalization of its glorious and wondrous implications which arouses the soul toward doxological adoration of the Holy One.

It is unlikely that the preacher of twenty-first century America will employ the poetic form of St. Ephraim, just as he is unlikely to model St. John Chrysostom's rhetorical style of oratory. However, as divine inspiration is infused with human imagination and creativity, such artistic skill can nonetheless emerge in preaching that is iconic — preaching that lifts the listeners beyond the literal meaning of words and text into the realm of transcendence. As Coniaris indicates, "According to Orthodox spirituality, the way to God is not primarily through the mind, but through the heart."[2] While the postmodern preacher may not craft homiletical hymns or classical oratory, he must still creatively and imaginatively incarnationalize the Gospel through the medium of human language in a manner that brings the transformative, eternal truths of the Good News from the mind of the listener into

---

[1] Old, *The Patristic Age*, 254.

[2] Coniaris, 50.

the deepest chambers of his heart. True Orthodox preaching is about moving the faithful ever toward union with God, not by means of peddling bare propositional truth, but by creating opportunities for intimate holy encounters assisted by the imaginative use of language.

> For just as religion is never merely a theological debate but always worship and obedience, so apostolic Christianity is never merely familiarity with the facts, but always union with the risen Christ....For what men heard, listening to the apostles, was not simply a human testimony: it was the self-testimony of the risen Jesus. They did not say, "This is the truth: we will learn it, and it will instruct us." They said, "This is the Lord: we have waited for Him, and He will save us."[1]

Burghardt insists, "I must shape my homily in such fashion — so carefully, so artistically, so imaginatively — that my congregation sees not so much me as Christ Jesus, that my listeners listen to what the Lord is saying to each individually."[2] So while it is necessary for us to communicate in a manner that connects with the listeners of our day, we must nonetheless appreciate the essential value of

---

1 Stewart, 46–7.

2 Burghardt, 185.

the artistic use of language in facilitating the spiritual goal of preaching; of bringing the listeners into an encounter with the Risen Lord and into union with God through Christ in the Holy Spirit.

The role of preaching in Orthodox spirituality is, of course, not solely dependent upon the preacher, but the preacher and his own spirituality is nonetheless critical within the dynamic of preaching and spirituality. Burghardt argues that one of the demands which homiletic imagination makes is "for a preacher who is aflame with the message he carries, who has himself been captured by the Christian story, enraptured by the Catholic vision...."[1] In short, the spirituality of preaching is mediated out of the spirituality of the preacher. Hopko states, "The saints teach us that those who do not pray and fast, who cannot be silent, both interiorly and exteriorly, and who do not engage in spiritual warfare with their passions and sins, must never speak — for they will have nothing to say."[2] While the preacher is also a broken soul on a journey to healing and wholeness, he nonetheless must be committed to a life of holiness and virtue. "Purity of the heart sees God, and anything that besmirches the purity of the soul spoils the vision. One of the prime pre-conditions of good preaching is daily contrition, sorrow, repentance

---

1 Ibid., 39.

2 Hopko, 178.

and confession in the life of the preacher."[1] In an age in which the cult of personality takes center stage in the preaching ministry of many churches, Orthodox spirituality demands something very different. "In a word, only those who are freed from the slavery of the vain imaginations of their own minds and hearts, and are liberated from their own versions of reality, can see and hear, and also therefore speak and preach God's Word. The Lord 'leads the humble in what is right, he teaches the humble his way' (Psalm 25.9)."[2] It is from the preacher's own humility and continual repentance by which his preaching will be ablaze with the Spirit of Christ, and by which his listeners will be brought to humility and true godly repentance; the condition by which broken souls are restored and union with God may begin.

Having examined how the artistic aspect of iconic preaching functions toward its spiritual end, and having acknowledged the critical need for the preacher to be in a state of spiritual health, we now consider the manner and means by which the preacher's homiletical art assists others toward spiritual health. In so doing, we must first see preaching as an aspect of worship which engages our entire being; our mind and our

---

1 Coniaris, 51.

2 Thomas Hopko, *Speaking the Truth in Love: Education, Mission, and Witness in Contemporary Orthodoxy* (Crestwood, New York: St. Vladimir's Seminary Press, 2004), 51–2.

heart, our rationality as well as our interior being, as indicated by Bishop Kallistos Ware:

> In our literal use of words we reach the reasoning brain; by means of poetry and music, of art, symbol and ritual act, we reach the other layers of the human personality. The one aspect of worship is as essential as the other. If our words possess no literal meaning — or if we recite or sing them in such a way as to render the meaning unintelligible — then our worship will degenerate into magic and mumbo jumbo, and will be no longer worthy of logical sheep. If, on the other hand, our worship is exclusively through words, interpreted literally and rationally, it may be true worship of the mind, but it will not yet be worship of the mind *in the heart*.[1]

This integration of rationality and artistic language within the context of worship strikes at how preaching supports Orthodox spirituality which, at its core, is about the unification of the mind (*nous*) and heart. Within Orthodox spirituality, the *nous* is understood to be the "energies" of the soul while the heart is the "essence" of the soul. In fallen humanity, the soul suffers disintegration. "The *nous* which is scattered outside and diffused through the senses into the world is sick,

---

1 Bishop Kallistos Ware, *The Inner Kingdom* (Crestwood, NY: St. Vladimir's Seminary Press, 2000), 63–4.

fallen, prodigal. It must return from it diffused state to the heart, and then be united with God."[1]

The artistic language of iconic preaching assists in the reintegration of mind and heart. It is the powerful illustration, the rightly chosen metaphor, the carefully crafted word image, the rhythm and rhyme of poetic language that takes captive the mind that is diffused and distracted with worldly thoughts and brings it to the heart, to the place of the Divine. Though the *nous*, in a strict Orthodox sense, is distinguished from reason (a function of the brain),[2] it nonetheless can become enslaved to rationality, a condition which is so prevalent in western Evangelical Christian theology. Robert Arnold describes this state of theological affairs:

> The Evangelical imagination could not, however, allow the doctrine of God's revelation to remain shrouded in mystery. The myriad of anchorites, monks, nuns, hierarchs, priests, and pious laymen throughout the ages were all content to declare the Bible God's written Word, to read it with the eyes of faith, and to live according to its instruction. The simple parish priest, whether in Rome or Constantinople, never gave a tinker's cuss whether the Bible could be proved inaccurate in any of its

---

1 Metropolitan Hierotheos of Nafpaktos, *Orthodox Spirituality*, trans. Effie Mavromichali (Levadia: Birth of the Theotokos Monastery, 1992), 38.

2 Ibid., 37.

historical or geographical assertions. The babushkas of Russia, that indomitable army of kerchiefed grandmothers who weep rivers of tears at the reading of the prayers, are wholly unaffected when a German scholastic pompously announces to the world that the Bible is rife with all sorts of scientific and moral inconsistencies. But the Evangelical, that poor little orphan of the Enlightenment, is not content to simply accept with his heart the Bible as God's loving message to lost humanity. He rather applies to it all the rational and analytical tools he can muster to make its message more acceptable to his very modern and scientific mind.[1]

Though human reason is a divine gift and certainly should be utilized in study, preaching, worship, and the pursuit of God; more than ever, the *nous* needs deliverance from its bondage to the rationalism of our age in order to "take every thought captive to obey Christ."[2] It is the imaginative, creative, iconic language of Orthodox preaching that may assist. The truth of the Gospel which is first apprehended by the mind and rationality of the listener must make a journey to the heart. It is the language of iconic preaching that

---

1 Robert Lloyd Arnold, *Orthodoxy Revisited: Contrasting the Faith and Practice of the Eastern Orthodox Church with Evangelical Doctrine* (Salisbury, Massachusetts: Regina Orthodox Press, Inc., 2005), 21–2.

2 2 Cor. 10:5, RSV.

facilitates that journey of truth, and in so doing, frees the *nous* from the heavy chains of rationalism and brings it to the heart, the interior being and essence of the soul. It is as the *nous* and heart are reunited, as the energies and essence of the soul become one, there abiding with Truth and the very presence of God, that spiritual healing is accomplished.

It is the intrinsic relationship between language and transcendence that enables Orthodox preaching to function in an anagogical sense, that is, in bringing the listener into the place of transcendence, into the very presence of God. As noted by Colt Anderson, "The anagogical sense uplifts the soul by presenting it with a vision of the joys of heaven. Since it points to the promise of glory, anagogy was tied to the virtue of hope."[1] Traditional Orthodoxy understands this from a contemplative, hesychastic approach, or *theōria* which brings one to a vision of God. To allow the creative and artistic language of iconic preaching quickened by the Holy Spirit to transport us from the rational level of the spoken word into the glorious heights (and depths) of the Divine is to heed the admonishment of Saint Paul, "Set your minds on things that are above, not on things that are on earth."[2] It is *theōria*, the contemplative vision of God, which serves as both the

---

[1]   C. Colt Anderson, *Christian Eloquence: Contemporary Doctrinal Preaching* (Chicago, IL: Hillenbrand Books, 2005), 5.

[2]   Col. 3:2, RSV.

beginning of preaching (in the preparation of the oral icon) and the end of preaching (in spiritually engaging the oral icon). As mind and heart are united by way of *theōria*, facilitated by iconic preaching, we find our true center and our place of healing and wholeness. Anything less misses the mark of true spirituality, as indicated by Archimandrite Zacharias, "The greatest misfortune for man is to remain without experience in mind and heart, that is, never to have tasted of God or to have received knowledge of Him."[1]

Finally, it is this anagogical sense of iconic preaching which abides as the spiritual goal of preaching: leading the faithful toward *theosis* and into union with God whereby we may become icons of God. As Orthodox preaching brings us to a place of transcendence, we begin to understand something about the nature of God's self-revelation. "This God reveals Himself as transcendent to every image which could make known His nature, but He does not refuse personal relationship, living intercourse with men, with a people; He speaks to them and they reply, in a series of concrete situations which unfold as sacred history."[2] As active participants

---

1 Archimandrite Zacharias, *Remember Thy First Love: The Three Stages of the Spiritual Life in the Theology of Elder Sophrony.* First American edition (Dalton, PA: Mount Thabor Publishing, 2010), 79.

2 Vladimir Lossky, *In the Image and Likeness of God*, ed. John H. Erickson & Thomas E. Bird (Crestwood, New York: St. Vladimir's Seminary Press, 1974), 129.

of sacred history through the concrete and particular circumstances of life in the Church, we continue in the spiritual course which God has ordained. And as we encounter divine transcendence, facilitated and mediated by Orthodox preaching, we begin to realize our true end. "Through baptism in the Church man can find his real being. In other words, the Church offers a cure and a healing, returning man to his natural state. And so man in the Church, participating in the life of the deity, himself becomes an icon."[1] To the extent that we open ourselves to the healing and deifying power of God is the extent by which we image the glory of God. It is the faithful and unyielding proclamation of the Gospel which assists in mediating this sanctifying grace. It is the imaginative and artistic preaching of the Good News, quickened and empowered by the Holy Spirit, which manifests as the oral icon of Christ. And it is from this holy encounter with our Lord that we too may become icons — icons of Christ for all the world to behold.

---

[1] Scouteris, 93.

Conclusion

This, beloved, is the preaching of the truth, and this is the character of our salvation, and this is the way of life, which the prophets announced and Christ confirmed and the apostles handed over (παραδίδωμι) and the Church, in the whole world, hands down (ἐγχειρίζω) to her children.

— Saint Irenaeus of Lyons,
On the Apostolic Preaching

The people of our postmodern world are dying a spiritual death. They feel the pangs of their own hunger and thirst, and yet in a neo-pagan culture of moral relativism and religious syncretism where every promise of fulfillment under the sun is pronounced, they remain in a wilderness of their own making. The court jester of entertainment and frivolity is ordered up time and time again. The escape proves only temporary. Boredom, aimlessness, and even despair are only one joke, one laugh, one emotional high, one thrill away. And so the world brings its insatiability to bear on any semblance of religious life. Where entertainment and delight may admittedly lack staying power, surely the esteemed doctors of academia may save the day with their science and scholarly rigor. But in the last analysis, neither showmanship nor scholasticism abides the pulpits of our churches where the Gospel of Christ is to be proclaimed with any integrity. Indeed the masses are hungry and thirsty for Truth. Yet not realizing the essence of their own need, they grope for counterfeits, settle for theological and moral pluralism, and are ultimately left empty and jaded, skeptical of anyone claiming to have answers. This is the culture in which we live, and while it certainly appears as rock-hard ground to till, we must conclude from this study that Orthodox preaching offers a unique opportunity to break the ground and to penetrate the hearts of such a people.

While we are hopeful that the faithful of our assemblies are certainly more spiritually astute than the secular society, thereby giving us easier ground to till, they nonetheless are largely the product of a highly visual and aural postmodern age that is bombarded with the unrelenting and ubiquitous images and sound bites of their televisions, computers, iPads, and smart phones. We would be naively mistaken to believe that we did not have to continually re-evangelize our own people of Faith, that we did not have to work hard to preach the Gospel in a manner that penetrated their own information and image overloads, and that met them exactly where the culture has "wired" them to be. It is Orthodox preaching as the oral icon of Christ which offers a compelling answer to the dilemma of our day. By crafting imaginative and creative word images of the Good News and presenting them to the faithful in the context of Eucharistic liturgical worship, not only are we able to compete with the other images and truth claims of the world, but we have the privilege of allowing the faithful to see Jesus. Walter Burghardt wrote, "Late in life I have begun to grasp why some pulpits confront the preacher graphically with the request of the Greeks to Philip: 'Sir, we would like to see Jesus' (Jn 12:21). How simple a request…and how stunning! Here is our burden and our joy: to help believing Christians to see Jesus — not with our eyes but with their own."[1] Our study has concluded that Orthodox preaching has the ability to do just this. And in so doing, we have also examined what it means for preaching to be iconic.

In Chapter 1 we surveyed the work of preparing the oral icon of Christ by means of the preacher's exegetical work of biblical interpretation through a Christological hermeneutic. This exegetical work is not accomplished purely through science and academic rigor, but through the divine-human work of discerning the spiritual sense of the text which is guided by the Spirit of Christ and informed by the sacred Tradition of the Church. It is the Church, the

---

1 Burghardt, 27.

Body of Christ, which remains the rightful ground of accurate biblical interpretation, and by which the exegete becomes an active participant in salvation history. The Christological hermeneutic of iconic preaching derives from the patristic methodologies of typology and *theōria*. It is typology which enables the exegete to perceive the entirety of salvation history as having its ground, coherence, meaning, movement, and end in God's self-revelation in the Incarnation and the salvific work of Jesus Christ. *Theōria* as the "soul" of Orthodox exegesis guides the preacher toward a spiritual sense of the text as made manifest through a contemplative and worshipful vision of God in Christ. It is therefore the patristic hermeneutic methodologies of typology and *theōria* by which the verbal icon of Christ presented in Scripture begins its translation and transformation into the oral icon of Christ through preaching.

Chapter 2 highlighted the sacramental nature of preaching within the context of the Divine Liturgy, the place of true iconic preaching. We examined how the symbiosis between Word and Sacrament derives from the Emmaus event with the Risen Christ and continues to be manifest in liturgical Orthodox preaching which remains grounded in Baptism and points to the Eucharist. The Liturgy is dependent on the Word of God, and yet, the Word of God proclaimed apart from the Eucharist and the liturgical life of the Church is incapable of fully mediating the presence of the Risen

Lord. It is the preached Word in symbiotic balance with the Sacraments that serves as the milieu of true Orthodox preaching which manifests as the oral icon of Christ.

Chapter 3 presented the revelatory art of preaching as the means by which divinely inspired word images of the Gospel make "visible" the Good News for the listeners and thereby mediate the presence of Christ. We examined how the parabolic preaching of Jesus abides as the archetypal method of inductive preaching. Congruent with the Incarnation and how we experience life inductively, we concluded how the inductive approach to preaching most effectively delivers the truth of the Gospel in a manner which inspires holy imitation. Through the utilization of artistic and imaginative word images, listeners are able to appropriate the truth for themselves and interpret the particular concrete circumstances of their lives in the light of the Gospel. Though homiletical style and form may vary across cultures and languages, we saw from our study of the preaching of St. John Chrysostom and St. Peter Chrysologus that the effective art of presenting the Gospel through creative and imaginative language remains a universal constant in iconic preaching. It is such artful preaching that creates the opportunity for a holy encounter with the Risen Lord whereby the listeners are moved toward godly repentance and true amendment of life.

In Chapter 4, we examined the role of preaching in Orthodox spirituality. Flowing from the prophetic witness of the Church is the anagogical sense of preaching which brings the listeners outside of the mere grammatical and literal meaning of language into the transcendent realm of the Divine signified by the sign and symbol of the spoken language. We saw how artistic and poetic language such as that employed in the homiletical hymns of St. Ephraim the Syrian may assist in leading the listener from a cognitive reception of the Gospel to an interior appropriation of the truth whereby the mind (*nous*) and heart may be reunited. As Orthodox preaching begins with *theōria* as a patristic hermeneutic methodology, so it ends with *theōria*. It is iconic preaching that lifts the listener into a hesychastic vision of God in Christ through the Holy Spirit, and moves the listener ever toward *theosis*, the goal of our salvation and sanctification, and the means by which we ourselves become icons of Christ.

Our study has revealed the iconic nature of Orthodox preaching including its faithfulness to the witness of Scripture and the apostolic and patristic Tradition of biblical interpretation, its integral connection to the sacramental and liturgical life of the Church, its creative and imaginative use of word images of the Good News, and its transcendence in support of the goal of Orthodox spirituality. It is such preaching that not only heralds the Gospel of the crucified, resurrected, and ascended Lord, but that truly mediates

His holy presence. Orthodox preaching as the oral icon of Christ therefore possesses the ability to connect with the people of our image-driven postmodern culture, to break through their own skepticism and to confront them with Him who can meet their greatest needs. It is not entertainment or emotionalism or moral philosophy or scholasticism which mediates the Gospel in all of its transformative power, but Jesus Christ Himself. It is Orthodox preaching which points to Jesus, and indeed gives them Jesus.

Finally, in acknowledging the foundational and essential importance of preaching in the Orthodox Christian faith and in our life of spirituality, preaching can never abide as an appendix to our Liturgy, but must remain integral to it. Additionally, we would never give aspiring iconographers crayons and little training and expect them to create "windows into heaven." Neither should we expect that a seminarian will graduate as a fine preacher if his theological education has provided only a modicum of training and education in preaching and the homiletic arts. The Church is called to be the visible presence of Christ in a lost and dying world, and if the Church's iconic preaching is a principal means of living out that call and effectively connecting with our postmodern society, then we need to be willing to invest more heavily in preaching excellence. Perhaps the time is ripe for a reassessment of the scope and breadth of homiletical education and training in our seminaries. The Church, and certainly the world, needs men who are given over to the work of the Gospel, men who not only know and love the Bible as the verbal icon of Christ, but men who also know how to preach it iconically. For it is through the work of creatively and faithfully translating the *verbal* icon into the *oral* icon of Christ that people will meet our Lord, and that the world, one soul at a time, will be transformed.

Bibiography

Allen, Joseph J. *The Ministry of the Church: The Image of Pastoral Care.* Crestwood, New York: St. Vladimir's Seminary Press, 1986.

Anderson, C. Colt. *Christian Eloquence: Contemporary Doctrinal Preaching.* Chicago, IL: Hillenbrand Books, 2005.

Andrejev, Vladislav. "Art and Religion: Creativity and the Meaning of Image from the Perspective of the Orthodox Icon." *Theology Today* 61 (2004): 53-66.

Arida, Robert M. "Second Nicaea: The Vision of the New Man and New Creation in the Orthodox Icon." *Greek Orthodox Theological Review,* 1987: 417-424.

Arnold, Robert Lloyd. *Orthodoxy Revisited: Contrasting the Faith and Practice of the Eastern Orthodox Church with Evangelical Doctrine.* Salisbury, Massachusetts: Regina Orthodox Press, Inc., 2005.

Bloom, Anthony. *Beginning to Pray.* Mahwah, NJ: Paulist Press, 1970.

Bobrinskoy, Boris. "The Icon: Sacrament of the Kingdom." *St. Vladimir's Theological Quarterly* 31, no. 4 (1987): 287-296.

—. *The Mystery of the Church: A Course in Orthodox Dogmatic Theology*. Translated by Michael Breck. Yonkers, New York: St. Vladimir's Seminary Press, 2012.

Breck, John. *The Power of the Word in the Worshipping Church*. Crestwood, New York: St. Vladimir's Seminary Press, 1986.

Burghardt, Walter J. *Preaching: The Art and the Craft*. Mahwah, New Jersey: Paulist Press, 1987.

Cantalamessa, Raniero. *The Mystery of God's Word*. Translated by Alan Neame. Collegeville, Minnesota: The Liturgical Press, 1994.

Chrysologus, Peter. *The Fathers of the Church, St. Peter Chrysologus, Selected Sermons, Volume 3*. Edited by Thomas P. Halton. Translated by William B. Palardy. Vol. 110. Washinton, DC: The Catholic University of America Press, 2005.

—. *The Fathers of the Church: Saint Peter Chrysologus, Selected Sermons and Saint Valerian Homilies*. Edited by Roy Joseph Deferrari. Translated by George E. Ganss. Vol. 17. New York: Fathers of the Church, Inc., 1953.

—. *The Fathers of the Church: St. Peter Chrysologus, Selected Sermons, Volume 2*. Edited by Thomas P. Halton. Translated by William B. Palardy. Vol. 109. Washington, DC: The Catholic University of America Press, 2004.

Chrysostom, John. *Nicene and Post-Nicene Fathers: Chrysostom: Homilies on First and Second*

Corinthians. Edited by Philip Schaff. Vol.
12. Peabody, Massachusetts: Hendrickson
Publishers, Inc., 1999.

—. *Nicene and Post-Nicene Fathers: Chrysostom:
Homilies on the Acts
of the Apostles and Epistle to the Romans.*
Edited by Philip Schaff. Vol. 11. Peabody,
Massachusetts: Hendrickson Publishers, Inc.,
1999.

—. "Paschal Homily." *Orthodox Wiki.* . http://
orthodoxwiki.org/Paschal_Homily (accessed
June 30, 2013).

—. *Six Books on the Priesthood.* Translated by Graham
Neville. Vol. 1. Crestwood, New York: St.
Vladimir's Seminary Press, 1964.

Clark, Timothy. "The Function and Task of Liturgical
Preaching." *St. Vladimir's Theological Quarterly*
45, no. 1 (2001): 25-53.

Congar, Yves M J. "Real Liturgy, Real Preaching."
Worship 82, no. 4 (2008): 310-322.

Coniaris, Anthony. *Preaching the Word of God.*
Brookline, Massachusetts: Holy Cross
Orthodox Press, 1983.

Craddock, Fred B. *As One Without Authority.* St.
Louis, Missouri: Chalice Press, 2001.

—. *Preaching.* Nashville: Abingdon Press, 1985.

Dabovich, Sebastian. *Preaching in the Orthodox
Church.* Rollinsford, NH: Orthodox Research
Institute, 2008.

DeBona, Guerric. *Fulfilled in Our Hearing: History and Method of Christian Preaching.* Mahwah, NJ: Paulist Press, 2005.

Ephraim the Syrian. *Nicene and Post-Nicene Fathers.* Edited by Philip Schaff, & Henry Wace. Translated by J. B. Morris. Vol. 13. Peabody, Massachusetts: Hendrickson Publishers, Inc., 1999.

Florovsky, Georges. *Bible, Church, Tradition: An Eastern Orthodox View.* Belmont, Massachusetts: Nordland Publishing Company, 1972.

Gregory Palamas. *Saint Gregory Palamas: The Homilies.* Edited by Christopher Veniamin. Translated by Christopher Veniamin. Waymart, PA: Mount Thabor Publishing, 2009.

Gregory the Great. *Ancient Christian Writers: St. Gregory the Great, Pastoral Care.* Edited by Johannes Quasten, & Joseph C. Plumpe. Translated by Henry Davis. Vol. 11. Mahwah, New Jersey: Paulist Press, 1978.

Hatzidakis, Emmanuel. *The Heavenly Banquet: Understanding the Divine Liturgy.* Columbia, MO: Orthodox Witness, 2008.

Hierotheos, Metropolitan of Nafpaktos. *Orthodox Spirituality.* Translated by Effie Mavromichali. Levadia: Birth of the Theotokos Monastery, 1992.

Hopko, Thomas. *Speaking the Truth in Love: Education, Mission, and Witness in Contemporary Orthodoxy*. Crestwood, New York: St. Vladimir's Seminary Press, 2004.

—. "The Liturgical Sermon." *St. Vladimir's Theological Quarterly* 41, no. 2-3 (1997): 175-182.

Irenaeus of Lyons. *Ante-Nicene Fathers: The Apostolic Fathers with Justin Martyr and Irenaeus*. Edited by Alexander Roberts & James Donaldson. Vol. 1. Peabody, Massachusetts: Hendrickson Publishers, Inc., 1999.

—. *On the Apostolic Preaching*. Translated by John Behr. Crestwood, NY: St. Vladimir's Seminary Press, 1997.

Isaac the Syrian. *The Ascetical Homilies of Saint Isaac the Syrian*. Revised Second Edition. Translated by Holy Transfiguration Monastery. Brookline: Holy Transfiguration Monastery, 2011.

Janowiak, Paul. *The Holy Preaching: The Sacramentality of the Word in the Liturgical Assembly*. Collegeville, Minnesota: The Liturgical Press, 2000.

Kesich, Veselin. *Orthodox Research Institute*. 2012. http://www.orthodoxresearchinstitute.org/articles/dogmatics/kesich_verbal_icon.htm (accessed July 16, 2013).

Lischer, Richard. *Theories of Preaching: Selected Readings in the Homiletical Tradition*. Durham, North Carolina: The Labyrinth Press, 1987.

Lossky, Vladimir. *In the Image and Likeness of God.*
Edited by John H. Erickson, & Thomas
E. Bird. Crestwood, New York:
St. Vladimir's Seminary Press, 1974.

Martin, Linette. *Sacred Doorways: A Beginner's Guide
to Icons.* Brewster, Massachusetts: Paraclete
Press, 2002.

McKeown, Robert E. "Preaching and Poetic Vision:
A Response to Dr. Willimon." *Worship* 50, no.
2 (1976): 110-115.

Miller, Charles E. *Ordained to Preach: A Theology and
Practice of Preaching.* Eugene, Oregon:
Wipf and Stock Publishers, 2003.

Mitchell, Margaret M. *The Heavenly Trumpet:
John Chrysostom and the Art of Pauline
Interpretation.* Louisville, Kentucky:
Westminster John Knox Press, 2002.

Nektarios the Wonderworker. *Christology.* Translated
by Saint Nektarios Greek Orthodox
Monastery. Vol. 2. Roscoe, NY: Saint
Nektarios Greek Orthodox Monastery, 2006.

Nikolaou, Theodor. "The Place of the Icon in the
Liturgical Life of the Orthodox Church."
Greek Orthodox Theological Review 35,
no. 4 (1990): 317-332.

Old, Hughes Oliphant. *The Reading and Preaching
of Scriptures in the Worship of the Christian
Church, The Biblical Period.* Vol. 1. Grand
Rapids, Michigan: William B. Eerdmans
Publishing Company, 1998.

—. *The Reading and Preaching of the Scriptures in the Worship of the Christian Church, The Patristic Age.* Vol. 2. Grand Rapids, Michigan: William B. Eerdmans Publishing Company, 1998.

Ouspensky, Leonid, and Vladimir Lossky. *The Meaning of Icons.* Translated by G.E.H. Palmer, & E. Kadloubovsky. Crestwood, New York: St. Vladimir's Seminary Press, 1982.

Ozoline, Nicholas. "The Theology of the Icon." *The Greek Orthodox Theological Review* 38, no. 1-4 (1993): 281-290.

Piper, John. *The Supremacy of God in Preaching.* Grand Rapids, MI: Baker Books, 2004.

Robinson, Haddon W. *Biblical Preaching.* Second Edition. Grand Rapids, Michigan: Baker Academic, 2001.

Satterlee, Craig Alan. *Ambrose of Milan's Method of Mystagogical Preaching.* Collegeville, Minnesota: The Liturgical Press, 2002.

Scouteris, Constantine B. *Ecclesial Being: Contributions to the Theological Dialogue.* Edited by Christopher Veniamin. South Canaan, PA: Mount Thabor Publishing, 2005.

Skudlarek, William. *The Word in Worship: Preaching in a Liturgical Context.* Nashville: Abingdon, 1981.

Stephanou, Eusebius A. *Sacramentalized But Not Evangelized.* Destin, Florida: St. Symeon the New Theologian Press, 2005.

Stewart, James S. *A Faith to Proclaim*. Vancouver, British Columbia: Regent College Publishing, 1953.

Tarazi, Paul N. *Orthodox Synthesis: The Unity of Theological Thought*. Edited by Joseph J. Allen. Crestwood, New York: St. Vladimir's Seminary Press, 1981.

Townshend, Todd. *The Sacramentality of Preaching: Homiletical Uses of Louis-Marie Chauvet's Theology of Sacramentality*. New York, New York: Peter Lang Publishing, Inc., 2009.

United States Conference of Catholic Bishops. *Fulfilled in Your Hearing: The Homily in the Sunday Assembly*. Washington, DC: United States Conference of Catholic Bishops, 1982.

Vasileios, Archimandrite. *Hymn of Entry: Liturgy and Life in the Orthodox Church*. Translated by Elizabeth Brière. Crestwood, New York: St. Vladimir's Seminary Press, 1984.

Vrame, Anton C. *The Educating Icon: Teaching Wisdom and Holiness in the Orthodox Way*. Brookline, Massachusetts: Holy Cross Orthodox Press, 1999.

Wallace, James A., ed. *Preaching in the Sunday Assembly: A Pastoral Commentary on Fulfilled in Your Hearing*. Collegeville, Minnesota: Liturgical Press, 2010.

Ware, Bishop Kallistos. *The Inner Kingdom*. Crestwood, NY: St. Vladimir's Seminary Press, 2000.

Wilken, Robert Louis. *The Spirit of Early Christian Thought: Seeking the Face of God.* New Haven & London: Yale University Press, 2003.

Willimon, William H. "Kierkegaard on Preachers Who Become Poets." *Worship* 49, no. 2 (1975): 107-112.

Wybrew, Hugh. *The Orthodox Liturgy: The Development of the Eucharistic Liturgy in the Byzantine Rite.* Crestwood, New York: St. Vladimir's Seminary Press, 2003.

Zacharias, Archimandrite. *Remember Thy First Love: The Three Stages of the Spiritual Life in the Theology of Elder Sophrony.* First American edition. Dalton, PA: Mount Thabor Publishing, 2010.

—. *The Enlargement of the Heart.* Edited by Christopher Veniamin. Dalton , PA: Mount Thabor Publishing, 2012.

—. *The Hidden Man of the Heart: The Cultivation of the Heart in Orthodox Christian Anthropology.* Edited by Christopher Veniamin. Waymart, PA: Mount Thabor Publishing, 2008.

BOOK ENDORSEMENTS

Contemporary scholars tell us that post-modern man needs experiences of God in order to believe in Him. God has given us all of our senses in order to encounter and understand Him. Father James Hamrick offers us a tradition of preaching that allows the art to present God to contemporary man through experiences. Hamrick shows how Church fathers in their preaching painted with words an icon of Christ that could be encountered and engaged. They called the listener to use all of his senses to encounter the living Word and be healed and changed by Him. This book offers the modern preacher the ancient skills of the Church. It allows us to rethink our art and share in Christ's own preaching ministry. This book is a tool that should be in the box of every Christian preacher.

— Bishop John Abdalah,
Diocese of Worcester and New England, Antiochian Orthodox Christian Archdiocese of North America

Father James Hamrick's treatise is a highly recommended study of preaching within the Orthodox Tradition, appropriate to our contemporary setting. Using the Icon as an analogy for the sermon, Father James moves from the preparation of the sermon as an "oral Icon" of Christ to the engagement with this Icon in the context of Liturgy, where it presents a vision of God to the people that, in the words of the author, calls for "godly repentance and true amendment of life." Again, I would say this approach is indeed *apropos* in "our highly visual and aural postmodern culture."

— Bishop Thomas Joseph, Diocese of Charleston,
Oakland and the Mid-Atlantic, Antiochian Orthodox Christian Archdiocese of North America

Father James is not a man "to put cushions under every elbow" (St. Gregory the Great, Pastoral Care). But his largely justified castigation of modern sermons is balanced by an inspirational programme for bringing us back to the good old Orthodox way. Teachers of the faith, young and old, Orthodox and non-Orthodox, need to hear what he has to say.

— Professor David Frost, Principal, The Institute for Orthodox Christian Studies, Cambridge University

Father Hamrick's book on preaching is truly a new and creative approach to sermon preparation and delivery. We do not use the term "new" here in our culture's superficial faddish sense, but new in the sense of presenting something true, old, and real that has been lost, but is here found and presented in a clear, direct, and powerful way. Preaching, if done as it was anciently taught, is a holy endeavor, like writing an icon, opening up to us Jesus Christ and His glory. Father James' meditation is a must read for those who desire to set hearts aflame through preaching.

— Father John Worgul, Ph.D.,
Pastoral Associate for Evangelization and Adult Formation, St. Joseph Catholic Community, Eldersburg, Maryland

Father Hamrick's work introduces a much-needed and accessible treatment of the place of preaching within Orthodox Church tradition—aptly likened to an oral icon. Evoking the rich heritage of Saint John Chrysostom, Saint Ephraim, Saint Peter Chrysologus, and other Church Fathers as illustrations of the elegant and often sublime artistic expression to which Orthodoxy is heir, we are urged to take up our tools in the manner of the iconographers to write, through word images, a place of holy encounter with the Divine. In this manner, Hamrick prescribes a fully Orthodox mode, uniquely distinct from much contemporary preaching that is especially characteristic of the Protestant traditions.

— John S. Jorgensen, Ph.D., Independent Scholar of Religion, Near Eastern Archaeology and History

BOOK COVER ICON

The icon which appears on the cover of the book is courtesy of Kenneth D. Dowdy, an Orthodox Christian convert, who has written icons since 1977. He studied with John Terzis, who apprenticed under the renowned Byzantine iconographer, Photios Kontoglou. Mr. Dowdy's work may be accessed at www.kennethdowdy.com.

www.orthodoxlogos.com

www.ingramcontent.com/pod-product-compliance
Lightning Source LLC
Chambersburg PA
CBHW020410130626
46549CB00006B/2508